AN UNFORGETTABLE RIDE

By Bill McDaniels

Arcane Publishing
Los Angeles, CA

Book design by Booknook.biz
Cover design by Goldin Productions
Illustrations by Krunislav Stojanovski

Names: Bill McDaniels, Author. | Chris Drabenstott, Writer. | Tracey McDaniels-Miller and Robert McDaniels, writers of Foreword.

AN UNFORGETTABLE RIDE

First printing, May 2020

Paperback ISBN: 978-1-7348638-0-2
Hardback ISBN: 978-1-7348638-2-6
Ebook ISBN: 978-1-7348638-1-9

Published in the United States of America

AN UNFORGETTABLE RIDE

BILL McDANIELS

Composed by International Best-Selling Litterateur,
Chris Drabenstott

Arcane Publishing, LLC
Los Angeles, CA

PRAISE

If you think you can't accomplish your dreams, Bill McDaniels will give you every reason why you can. Bill, thank you for being my inspiration.

—*Suzanne Pucci, President and CEO,*
Stanley Steemer, Columbia, SC

I have known Bill for the past 10 years, and I am his golf buddy. They say you can judge a man's character by playing golf with him. Now, I'm able to understand his fierce, competitive nature and his take-no-prisoners approach to life. I am also his doctor, so I can claim I know him inside and out. After I read his life story, I immediately wanted to hug him. What a journey! This reminds me of Lord Buddha in his quest for enlightenment: he went to look for a job in his twenties. The prospective employer asked him about his qualifications. He promptly replied, "I can think, I can wait, and I can fast." This implied that he was intelligent, he had patience, and he could self-sacrifice. These characteristics embody my friend, Bill. It's been an honor knowing you, and I look forward to growing old with you with young hearts and minds.

—*Raj Vasudeva MD, FACG,*
Consultants in Gastroenterology, Columbia, SC

What an amazing story of how to make the most of life rather than making excuses! I believe it will inspire others to make wiser, more intentional choices for themselves, and to live in such a way as to make life better for their community and every person with whom they cross paths. I can tell you from my friendship with Bill, this is how he lives, and this is genuinely who he is—a man leaving the world better than he found it.

—*Jimmy Currence, Pastor,*
GraceLife Church, Columbia, SC

I have known Bill McDaniels as a friend for over two decades, in both difficult times and on calm waters. When faced with a choice between doing the right thing on one hand and taking the easy way out on the other, he inevitably choses to be fair. It's just a part of who he is. For those who say that the American Dream is falling by the wayside, one need look no further than Bill McDaniels to see that it is strong, viable, and driving forward.

—Warren Moise, Lawyer,
Grimball and Cabaniss, Charleston, SC

What a terrific book! It not only outlines Bill's incredible journey from poverty to a successful businessman, but more importantly, it teaches many valuable life lessons. I've known Bill for over 20 years and I can testify that he lives his life just as he describes: as a hard-working man with honesty, integrity, a positive attitude, and with love for his family and community. Oh, and did I mention, a sharp dresser!? Congratulations on all your success, Bill. You deserve it!

—John R. Mullins, First Vice President,
Truist Bank, Atlanta, GA

Some people (although, very few) make things happen, some people watch things happen, and others wonder, 'What just happened?' Bill definitely makes things happen. He's always on the lookout for an opportunity, whether it's a business deal or a charity function. When he's in, he's 100% in, and that's why he wins more than most people.

—Keith Shealy, Senior Vice President,
Truist Bank, Atlanta, GA

DEDICATION

To my mother, Rosalyn Russ McDaniels. Your selfless generosity and passion for humankind has been the example I've been inspired to emulate throughout my entire life. At only 4'10" tall, to me, you were, and always will be, a giant. I thank God for you.

CONTENTS

FOREWORD

Bill's unique optimism and perseverance were forged in a furnace of want and desperation that I have fortunately eluded. Seeing it all laid out in *An Unforgettable Ride* documents his journey in fresh detail for me, even though I've been in the back seat for over half the trip. His is a classical American story of rags to riches. He's brought his faith and industriousness from the sandhills of the rural Pee Dee and repurposed them to make better lives for countless employees, friends, and family members along the way. In the final analysis, it will be his enrichment of others (in a non-material sense) that will be his lasting legacy—a legacy far from being completed. I would only modify one thing in this book: Bill asserts, "Where you currently are = your starting point + the sum of your past decisions." For me, "Where you currently are = your starting point + the sum of your past decisions + Bill McDaniels." Pride may be a sin, but I can't help but be proud that Bill McDaniels is my father.

—*Rob McDaniels*

My father and I have recently returned from a three-day National Automotive Dealers Association (NADA) event in Las Vegas. Most of the people in our organization have the opportunity to see my father in his element, and how he makes the most out of every opportunity, but it's safe to say they have no clue the amount of time and energy he burns through in any given day. He is definitely a force to be reckoned with and has always been recognized as such.

At a very young age, he was cognizant of his circumstances yet keenly aware of the vision he had for his life. He simply had to find the vehicle to accelerate his journey. I may not have had him in my life much as a young child, but I learned many lessons from him about family that have carried me through to truly valuing the time I have with him now. Even loss has value because the choices made on the other side reflect the person. He was always a man that did the best he could with the tools he was given. He's a powerhouse in most aspects and a work in progress in others, but he is 100% human; when he makes mistakes and falls, he sees no other choice than to pick himself up and keep right on going. He has never expected anyone to give him any of the success he has rightfully achieved.

When I meet an old friend or acquaintance who has been in the business with him since way back when, they always tell me, "Oh, I just love your father. He is such a good man." I listen to count-less stories of their experiences together and of how he's helped so many people. I know he wants to live at least another 30 years, and I also know that when he's called home, he will be happy, but he may negotiate the terms.

—*Tracey McDaniels-Miller*

INTRODUCTION

"Every choice carries a consequence. For better or worse, each choice is the unavoidable consequence of its predecessor. There are not exceptions. If you can accept that a bad choice carries the seed of its own punishment, why not accept the fact that a good choice yields desirable fruit?"

—*Gary Ryan Blair*

WHO'S IN THE DRIVER'S SEAT, ANYWAY?

Without question, everything that has ever been achieved started with a thought and was followed by a choice to act on it. We're all faced with situations in life that require us to make choices—some are easy, some are a little tougher. The "easy" decisions typically happen on an unconscious level, without having to give them much thought at all. For instance, what suit I put on in the morning is a decision that I make based on things like the season of the year, what the weather forecast is for the day, and where I might be going. Although there's not a whole lot of push and pull happening here, I'm still making a choice between the gray pinstripe or the black three-button. It's a choice!

The decisions that seem to be the most difficult are the ones that require a little deeper level of thought; like where you should go to college, what career path you should follow, and even whether or not you should get married and start a family. All of these are thought of as "big" decisions because they're life changing. They shape who we are; more importantly, they can alter the course of our future.

I believe that God has a plan for all of us, but He also gives us choices, which either move us toward certain opportunities or away from them; if you're prepared when that door of opportunity opens, you can turn them into something really special.

As I reflect back on my life, I can pinpoint having made many "good" decisions that set me on the course to achieving success. One decision at a time, I began to see how my life was unfolding according to the decisions I was making, for better, and sometimes, for worse. There were some decisions that affected my success in a negative way, and others that catapulted me forward in ways I couldn't have imagined. So, you might be wondering, "How can you know ahead of time if a decision is going to be a good one or a bad one?" After all, none of us have a crystal ball, and, as humans, we certainly don't have the omniscient mind of God. To be honest, even if we *could* see the future, we'd miss out on the ability to learn from our decisions and use our valuable life lessons to grow to be better people. We'd eliminate the beautiful element of surprise that comes from God's infinite web of possibility. Personally, that's just not something I'm interested in doing. I've actually quite enjoyed the surprises along the way, and I still do.

As I considered writing this book, my primary objective was to help others by sharing my own personal experiences in many facets of life. Why do I think that my experiences can help you? The answer is, throughout my life, I've developed a deep understanding about the power of decision making and how it can set you on a path to struggle and strife or to living a life that exceeds your wildest dreams.

In the following pages, I'll be sharing the lessons I've learned from the decisions I made as a child growing up in extreme poverty, as a young man working to put food on the table for myself and my family, as an eager businessman trying to make my way in car sales, as a husband and father raising children and building houses, as a successful business owner and leader, as a philanthropist serving my community, and as a Christian, striving to live my life on a higher, more spiritual level. All of these experiences included decisions that taught me something valuable. As you navigate these pages, you will naturally be taken on a journey— my journey. It includes my routes, detours, and destinations; although it is not designed to lead you in any certain direction, it is designed to challenge you to question where you are now, how you got there, where you want to be, and most importantly, who you want to become. This isn't one of those books that you speed through with the pedal to the metal; it's quite the opposite. My sincere hope is that this book will cause you to pump the brakes and slow down long enough to extract some of the wisdom that may help you make better decisions in your own life that lead you on a ride where you experience more success, more love, and ultimately, more happiness.

My second objective in writing this book was to leave a trace of my life for my family. Next to your relationship with God, I believe the relationships you have with family are the most important ones you can have, and in so many ways, my family is the foundation for this book.

Before we begin this ride together, I think it's important to say a bit more about decisions because we'll be referring back to some of the key principles and ideas throughout the book. There's actually a lot more that goes into making decisions than you might think.

CHECKING THE REARVIEW MIRROR

One of the biggest factors that has directed my life path is being able to learn from my past mistakes. Have you ever noticed that it always seems easier (and a little more fun) to share your big moments of glory rather than the times you fell flat on your face? The truth is that some of the biggest and most valuable lessons in my business came when I failed to win over a customer or fell short of hitting my projected targets. I learned so much more from those moments as I reflected back on the steps that led to the disappointment because I knew for certain that if I made the right changes, the next time, I could come out on top.

Learning from your mistakes is absolutely necessary if you want to reach your highest level of success. You can't be afraid to make mistakes, and you definitely can't be afraid to use them as your biggest ally. Every mistake is an opportunity to grow; failure can be your biggest teacher if you approach it that way. Learning from past mistakes is your key to creating more success in your profession and in your life. As you'll see, I'm living proof of that.

ANTICIPATING THE CURVES

I remember when I got my first car. More than anything, I just wanted to go fast! It was such a rush to be cruising down the open road with my whole life in front of me. One thing about a smooth ride is that you have to develop the ability to anticipate what's coming. For instance, if you're approaching a sharp curve, you actually have less control over the car when your eyes are focused on the road that's immediately in front of you versus fixing your vision much further ahead. Did you know that? When you're hugging a curve at a fast speed, you have to direct your focus further into the distance to experience a smoother ride.

The same thing goes for decisions and consequences: always looking for and anticipating the unexpected will help you see the potholes before you actually hit them. The consequences of our choices are directly related to the decisions that we make, and oftentimes, people think they can make bad decisions and escape the consequences. They want someone to rescue them from their bad choices rather than take personal responsibility for them. There's a natural human desire to be delivered from the consequences of something that we actually had some control over. Take, for instance, people who have incurred large amounts of debt and then seek to be delivered from the obligation of repayment through bankruptcy, or those who seek deliverance from a disease by taking a pill to treat the symptoms rather than taking certain steps to change the unhealthy behaviors that caused the symptoms in the first place. No matter how hard we try, we cannot avoid or escape consequences; they will always tell the true story behind our decisions.

TAKING OWNERSHIP

There is great power in being able to make our own choices. We can choose what kind of life we want to live and what type of person we want to be. We aren't just a result of how our parents treated us or a product of our environment; we are a result of the choices we make every day, and those choices start with knowing what you want and what you don't want out of your life. This might seem like an elementary concept, but the reality is, most people have no clue where they are in life, where they're headed, or how they're going to get where they want to go because they haven't taken the time and effort to sit down and map it out. And the trouble is, by not choosing what you want, you're unconsciously betting on "the luck of the draw" and living by happenstance rather than by your own conscious creation. Leaving life up to chance is the way that many Americans spend their days, which, sadly, means relinquishing your God-given power to take hold of the wheel and steer yourself in whatever direction you want to go.

Of course, we all drift from time to time—unplanned events and disturbances in life happen to all of us. You can find yourself suddenly and unexpectedly spinning out of control, but the key is to recognize what caused you to veer off course, recover from it, and get yourself right back on track. In the car business, we call that course-correction. Although you don't always have control over the circumstances in life, you do have control over your reactions and responses to them. And that's what builds a strong character. You can choose to sit on the shoulder or get right back into the driver's seat, buckle up, and keep going.

If you don't know where you're going, don't waste your gas.

By taking ownership of your life and being accountable for the decisions you've made, you can absolutely change your life for the better, no matter how old or young you are. You can make the choice to be happy and make a decision to respond positively to all of life's situations. You can take control and be a victor instead of becoming a victim.

You can choose whether you *reflect* or *affect* your environment.

You can choose to be happy or not, regardless of what you have or don't have.

You can choose how you respond to hard times, with positivity or negativity.

You can choose to take responsibility for your actions or blame others for your failures.

I want to challenge you to take an honest self-assessment. What choices are you currently making in your life? Are they ones that result in positive outcomes or negative consequences? Are you putting forth the effort required to make changes in the areas you need to? If not, what is the cost that's associated with sitting idle and avoiding change? Will you make less money? Have poorer health? Experience turbulent relationships?

Consider the short and long-term results of your choices and look for ways to learn from your past decisions. There's nothing you can do to alter what has happened in the past, so dwelling on what went wrong is futile. What you *can* do is change how you choose to think about your past circumstances and decide to take full responsibility for how you responded to them. This takes courage, commitment, and determination—and no one can do it for you.

KNOWING WHEN TO YIELD

Timing is everything. One thing I've learned is that my timing and God's timing don't always line up. In fact, there have been specific times in my life where I've prepared for certain milestones, only to realize more setbacks. Why? Because sometimes you can get out of alignment with God's timing when you're focused on your own, and you ignore your intuition—that quiet, inner voice that gives you a hunch as to which route to take when you approach a fork in the road. Accessing and utilizing the power of intuition means developing an awareness of what is happening in the body as well as the mind, and this aspect is vital for making excellent decisions.

I'm sure you've heard phrases like "I have a gut feeling," or "My heart is telling me…," or "I should've listened to my first mind." This is your intuition trying to bring you into awareness as to which way you should go. It's your instinct, your sixth sense. These gut feelings are your personal, internal signals that let you know how to make a good decision instead of a bad one. But you have to learn to listen to it, trust it, and follow it. It's the best GPS you've got.

Checking the experiences that are in your rearview mirror also contributes to developing a stronger intuition because those experiences either ended well or maybe not so well, and you can assess what worked and what didn't. The more experiences you have and the better you've internalized what worked in your favor and what didn't, the better your ability will be to choose the right option moving forward. I love this story about decisions:

"Sir, what is the secret of your success?", a reporter asked a company president.
　　"Two words."
　　"And, sir, what are they?"
　　"Good decisions."

"And how do you make good decisions?"

"One word."

"And sir, what is that?"

"Experience."

"And how do you get experience?"

"Two words."

"And, sir, what are they?"

"Bad decisions."

(Anonymous)

Everyone is born with intuition, but it takes practice to recognize your inner voice when it's talking to you, and even more importantly, to trust it enough to follow its guidance.

TAKING THE SCENIC ROUTE

When I was growing up, as more people continued to buy cars, it was common for families to pile in and go for a Sunday drive. The goal wasn't to get from Point A to Point B as quickly as possible; rather, it was completely the opposite. There was value in taking a longer, more scenic route, just for the sake of experiencing something different and more beautiful. In life, we sometimes lean toward making decisions that are faster, easier, and more convenient than ones that take more effort and conscious planning. Don't get me wrong, there are times when making a quick decision is necessary; at the same time, we can learn a great deal by taking the time to really reflect on where we've been and what got us to where we are today.

In writing this book, I chose to take the scenic route. I chose to start from the beginning and retrace my steps through the decisions I've made in more than seven decades of life that have led me to experience some pretty unforgettable moments. Many who are reading this know the man behind McDaniels Auto Group, but my hope is that by taking you on this ride with me, you'll get a glimpse of where I've come from, where I've been, and where I've yet to go.

Thank you for coming along to experience the unforgettable ride of my life.

CHAPTER 1

THE STARTING LINE

YOUR STARTING POINT in life matters a lot. You might've been born with good genes or maybe not so good ones. You might've been born into a rich family or a poor one. You might've been raised in a dysfunctional environment or a fairly healthy one. These are all things you don't choose. You didn't choose your talents, skin color, or parents. You didn't even choose your own name. Your starting point, where you began living your life, matters—not because it predetermines where you're going to go in life; rather, it's always there to reflect back on to show you how far you've come.

You really have nothing to say about where and to whom you are born, and you have no influence on how lucky you will be in your life or what breaks you're going to catch along the way. Fortunately, there's another part of the equation to help define where you're headed in life—it's the sum of your past choices. Just take a look at some of your past choices and the decisions you've made, and then look at where you are now! No matter where you start, with time, good choices lead to a better life and bad choices lead to a lower quality of life. We make choices constantly, on both a conscious and unconscious level, and they have a big impact on how life turns out… probably more than you even realize.

In addition to your starting point, there's something called recalibration that's also a factor in determining how your life unfolds. We can all relate to having a stroke of luck that has nothing to do with our efforts. We can experience different situations where we gain a lot with investing only a small amount. You could win the lottery off of a $5.00 ticket; it's not likely, but you could. Your friend could get a fancy job and hire you, paying you triple your worth, even though your skills don't necessarily match up with the job. The first person you fall in love with could be your lifelong soul mate—the perfect fit for you, saving you from having to navigate through unhealthy relationships or failed marriages. These recalibrations are more or less out of your control; and let's be honest—they don't happen all that often, so you can't count on them.

Where you currently are = your starting point + the sum of your past decisions.

My starting point was in the small town of Mullins in Marion County, South Carolina. Mullins was founded in 1872, and by 1878, there were a whopping 75 inhabitants—12 families, to be exact. In the last century and a half, the population has only grown to about 4,500, and the town continues to sit on only three square miles of land. The employment rate, school system performance, housing market, and crime rate are among the worst in the country, and certainly in the state of South Carolina. In the beginning, there were only three stores and four unpaved streets; as a young child, I can still remember what a big deal it was when the dirt road of Highway 9 was paved. What a difference that made for hooking up the mule and wagon just to get a few groceries. Growing up in rural SC was a real struggle.

By 1894, the growth and sale of tobacco sparked the development of the city, and at one time, it was the largest tobacco-producing/marketing industry in the United States. Tobacco and farm life were the lifeblood of the community, so you can guess what the vocation of my family was… we were tobacco farmers. We also grew some corn and cotton but cultivating the two family farms of tobacco was pretty much how we lived life.

In 1947, I was born to Cromer Andrew McDaniels and Rosalyn Russ. I had an older brother, John, then came my older sister, Lorraine, who changed her name to Laura. I also had an older brother, Cleveland, who died when he was only six months old. Then there was me and my fraternal twin brother, Bobby, who passed away in 1984. Because we had that special twin bond, Bobby and I did just about everything together. And finally, I had a baby sister, Mary, who passed away in 2019.

Mother and Daddy were married on December 5th, 1938; she was 19, and he was 24. They met at the local fair, and my mother was under the impression that Daddy must've been pretty wealthy because he had one thing that not many people had at the time—a car! But let me tell you, Daddy's family was by no means rich. They had very little education—most only to about the third grade—and it wasn't long before she found out that that car wasn't his; it belonged to his parents. My daddy was a heavy drinker, but he was also a smooth operator when he was drinking, and I think Mother thought she could change him in more ways than one. Mother had graduated from high school, which was in 11th grade back then, and she was the eldest of 13 siblings.

TWO DRIVES, TWO MARRIAGES

Daddy was actually at that fair on a Friday night with another girl, but Mother caught his eye, and having already thrown back his fair share of "liquid courage," he walked straight over to her, chest puffed out, and told her that he wanted to come see her on Sunday. Sure enough, he showed up to meet my mother's parents two days later.

At the time, my maternal grandfather was a shoe salesman, and believe it or not, that company is still in business today. He traveled a lot selling shoes and would be gone for six weeks at a time, which made it that much harder for my grandmother to raise their 13 children. My grandfather also struggled with alcoholism, so when he first met my daddy, let's just say he wasn't too fond of him; when he looked at Daddy, he saw himself, and that wasn't the kind of man he wanted for his daughter.

Nevertheless, after meeting Mother's parents, Daddy took her out for a drive and then brought her back home. The following Sunday, he came back to see her again. That's when Mother looked at Daddy and said, "Cromer, my father does not like you, and he doesn't want me to ever see you again." And my daddy, who'd been drinking, of course, looked back at her and said, "You know what? I'm going to marry you tomorrow." Whether it was out of love at first sight or sheer rebellion, I'm not quite sure, but they were married the next day at the courthouse in Conway, SC. He never took mother back home to get any clothes or anything. My grandparents didn't even know about the wedding until the following Sunday when Mother and Daddy returned home to Mother's parents' house.

Daddy had a younger brother, Winston, and on that same Sunday, Winston asked my daddy if there were any other women in the house, and he replied, "There's a whole house full of girls!" (Truth be told, I think Winston may have come along for moral support 'cause Daddy knew what he might be in for after he told Mother's parents that he'd gone off and married their daughter.)

So, Mother, Daddy, and Winston all hopped in the car and went to break the news to Mother's parents. After getting there, Winston took a liking to one of Mother's sisters, Opal, and he took her out for a drive and brought her back home. The following Sunday, he came back and took her for another drive, but this time, he didn't bring her back home; they were married the next day. So, exactly two weeks after Mother and Daddy were married, Winston and Opal followed suit. Now, I grant you, this may sound a little hard to believe, but you have to remember that back then, most people didn't have the means to travel more than about 25 miles away from home, so when it came to relationships, the pickings were pretty slim.

After Mother and Daddy were married, they lived in a little town called Floyds, SC with Daddy's parents. There really wasn't a whole lot out there besides farming. The house they lived in had no running water and no bathroom, just an outhouse. The house was destroyed in 1954 by Hurricane Hazel. For food, they killed the livestock in the fall to have meat throughout the winter, and they grew sweet potatoes that were kept under a sort of teepee to be protected from the winter frost.

As kids, we'd play in those sweet potato teepees. Come to think of it, there was a lot of that—making our own fun. There wasn't much choice in how to spend our time. We couldn't afford bicycles or toys. As a matter of fact, I can only remember getting a red, rubber fire truck one Christmas. I believe it cost 39 cents, and I was told that was my Christmas present and I'd have to share it with my brother. There were no Christmas trees, and we really didn't celebrate any of the major holidays in a traditional way because we didn't have the money. There were a few years where we had a cut-down pine tree with popcorn strung around it and one string of lights. Some oranges, apples, and walnuts in a bag was a typical present from my aunts and uncles, and I was grateful for it. When school let out for the summer, there were no family vacations to look forward to. The extent of our recreation was playing stickball and swimming in the Pee Dee River, and that only happened when I wasn't working on the neighbors' tobacco farms five days a week, just to be able to buy my own clothes, which I'd have to wear a couple days in a row. Growing up, I struggled for every dime, and in the process, I learned the value of that dime.

NO NEED FOR A SUNDAY DRIVE

When it comes to my mother, I know if she could've given us more, she would've. She had a heart of gold and never met a stranger. I like to think I inherited those traits from her. After finishing high school and having five children, she went to work in a textile mill where she folded t-shirts and probably made all of $25-30 per week. And if she wasn't at home cooking and cleaning for us kids, you could bet she was in church. Unlike Daddy, Mother didn't drink at all and she was in church all the time, which meant so were we. Most kids might think that having to go to church so much would be a nuisance, but I actually quite preferred the safety inside those church walls to the drama and fighting that were so prevalent at home. Church was really the only place I felt safe because I knew nothing bad could happen to me there.

Every Sunday morning, Sunday night, and Wednesday night, Mother and I were at Free Welcome Pentecostal Holiness Church. It was a small church that wasn't more than a stone's throw to an old, abandoned schoolhouse—and that schoolhouse was our home. There was no need to take a Sunday drive to church because it was literally right across the street.

On any given Sunday, there might've been 35-40 people in that church, maybe 50 on Easter, Mother's Day, or Christmas. I was on the painting crew and the cleaning crew, dusting pews and sweeping floors. Church gave us something to do because we had no radio or TV. We had no stereo, no music to listen to. We were living in that schoolhouse that had been built in the '30s, so there were just a bunch of empty rooms, no bathroom or kitchen. The windows had been knocked out of the windowpanes, so we put up plastic on the outside to try to keep the wind out. The problem was, there were knot holes in the wall boards, so you could actually see straight through to the outside. There was no heat and no electricity, just oil lamps. There was also no running water, just a water pump outside and an outhouse. Until the age of 15, that's how I lived. Sometimes I wonder how I survived it.

My father never went to church with us much. He was a very kind person when he wasn't drinking, but as I look back, I honestly think he was drunk more days than he was sober. I think he had a lot of pride when he wasn't drinking but he never said a whole lot. I believe the alcohol was the only escape he had from the hard life he was living.

Times were tough back then. He knew he was trapped, and without an education, he didn't have much choice to do any better. There was no silver lining where he could be successful—at least, he didn't see one. He wasn't very strict, and he let us get away with a lot when he was sober. Mother... well, she was a different story. She was the disciplinarian of the two, and she wouldn't hesitate to keep us in line. When I was in trouble, she'd send me out to get a switch off the tree, and I can still hear her saying, "It better be a good one!"

Mother really did try her best to make sure we had what we needed. She handmade our mattresses out of fertilizer bags and stuffed them with cotton. She cut up our clothes to make quilts, and she sewed all of our shirts because there was nowhere near enough money to buy our clothes from a store. If we wore through a pair of shoes, we'd have to go barefoot until the Fall when we could get a new pair for school. Our kitchen table was more like an old picnic table and we'd sit around it on wooden crates. She was a special angel and worked her butt off trying to keep it all together as best as she could.

As it turned out, Mother carried most of the parenting load, as Daddy hardly ever worked because of his binge drinking. There were many nights that I sat and cried because I knew she didn't want this life for her children. I think it was agonizing for her, and she cried a lot over it. Our house was rarely a peaceful place, especially on the weekends. Between my daddy and his drinking buddies, it was inevitable that after a little too much moonshine, a brawl would break out; over what, I'm not sure.

Daddy got his temper honest; his mother was a pistol. She was all of about five feet tall, weighed about 90 pounds, had the frame of a stick, and was tough as nails. She would have a baby in the morning and chop cotton in the afternoon! And when those drunken brawls would get started, if she was in earshot, she'd jump right in there with them to try to break it up by using a hammer to knock them in the head to get their attention. There was no shortage of drama. You're supposed to have fun as a child but instead, we were learning how to live a life full of misfortune and dysfunction. But it really wasn't anyone's fault. Neither of my father's parents had more than about a third-grade education, and having eight kids was mostly for the purpose of having a

Free Welcome Pentecostal Holiness Church

workforce to man the farms, which wasn't uncommon back then. Everyone was just doing the best they knew how.

As for my education, I spent about eight years of my young life attending school in Floyds. For most that time, I didn't have the 20 cents to buy lunch at school, so I'd either go without or, occasionally, bring a jelly biscuit with me. I fell behind the other kids my age and was forced to repeat the second grade because I came down with an uncontrollable fever for about three weeks, and my illness continued to get more and more severe. After about a month of being sick and unable to attend school, my illness had progressed to the point where I could barely walk. Mother finally took me to the town doctor, and he was unable to determine a diagnosis. He thought I might've contracted polio but couldn't be sure. Knowing that my mother was a religious woman and seeing the fear in her eyes, I remember the doctor telling her, "The only thing I can do is pray with you." So, that's what they did; after about five minutes, I was able to stand up and walk! I've never forgotten that moment and the power of prayer.

GUESSING ENGINES

As a child, I was always infatuated with cars. Our idea of fun would be sitting on the front porch on Highway 9 with eyes closed, playing "Name That Car." Using only our ears, we would guess what the make and model was just by the sound of the engine passing by. I got pretty good at that game, able to tell if it was a four or six-cylinder and even what year it was. "That was a '55 Chevy V-8!" I suppose that's where my fascination with cars began. There weren't all that many cars on the road back then because between 1941-1946, they stopped manufacturing them so they could convert the auto factory assembly lines into production facilities to build jeeps and tanks for the war. The prices

1957, age 10

for cars went through the roof, and few people could afford to buy them.

For as much as I remember about my childhood, there's probably an equal amount that I've forgotten and maybe even blocked out. I recognized at a very young age that my parents felt trapped in their circumstances but I knew deep down that I couldn't continue to live this way. I decided early on that I would never be trapped. I knew there was a better way to live, and I was determined to find it.

CHAPTER 2

REROUTING...

ONE THING I KNOW for sure is that you can't stop your life from changing. Sometimes it takes a decade for you to really figure out what life's all about, what you want to accomplish, and what you couldn't care less about. It only took me a little over a decade to realize that the extreme poverty I was raised in wasn't going to get me anywhere, but that didn't mean I knew how to change it.

In 1962, my older brother John made the decision to leave his job at the Mullins Textile Mill in search of a new career and a new life. I suppose he was the trailblazer when it came to making big decisions, having the courage to trade in the life we were living for something better. When he was only seven years old, Daddy had him working the farm, planting cotton, corn, and tobacco. As a young teenager, he too knew that being tied down to the farm and to that desperate town wasn't the kind of life he wanted. There were other people all around us who were "having things," and he was the first one to really question why we couldn't have some of those things, too. Our parents weren't making it any easier for us, that was for sure. Married and with a child on the way, John packed up and moved to the furniture capital of Thomasville, North Carolina and got a job working as a technician at the Thomasville Water Department. He had gotten out.

John had been in Thomasville for a while, and he came back home to visit us. The family dysfunction was so bad; I was doing my best just to survive. When John saw how volatile things were, he asked me if I wanted to come live with him. Even though I was just a teenager at the time, deep down, I knew that if I stayed, I would eventually end up just like everyone else. I also knew I wanted to make something of my life that I could be really proud of, and in my bones, I knew it couldn't be done in that desperate South Carolina town. Eventually, I would have to get out, and when John

With my brother, John

asked me to come live with him, "eventually" had finally arrived. It was 1963 and I was only 15 years old. John had rerouted; now it was my turn. I was about to leave the rest of my family and trade in the experiences of my childhood for a better life, and I hadn't even made it to high school yet. I made the decision—a big decision—that would change the course of my entire life.

I had saved up enough money for a bus ticket (which cost $1.25 back then) by pulling corn stalks for three days straight. I had made a whopping $3.00, and I was on a mission to make my move to a new life. I boarded the bus with the pair of blue jeans I was wearing, a pair of shoes, two pairs of socks, and a couple pairs of underwear. When I got to Thomasville, there was about a foot of snow on the ground and I didn't even have a coat. I don't even remember having a toothbrush. What I do remember is that it was the first place I had ever lived that had a toilet and a bathtub. As far as I was concerned, my decision was already paying off!

One thing about John… he and my daddy had something in common: they both loved to party. He would tell you he had a wild streak in him, which probably kept us apart more than I would've liked because I didn't want to be around some of the things he was caught up in. And he knew that. Still in his early twenties at the time, there was plenty of partying on the weekends, but that didn't stop him from helping me and taking me in. In a way, he saved my life, and I'll always be grateful to him for that.

Over the years, like many siblings do, we've gone through periods of falling out of touch; but one thing I know for certain is that John would do anything for me, as I would for him. John has said he doesn't know what would've happened if he had stayed in SC; he doesn't even like to think about it. I guess we're the same in that respect. Once we left, going back was never an option for either one of us.

About 18 months after I moved, Mother followed us to Thomasville, but she came by herself. At first, Daddy dug his heels in and refused to come with her, but after about a month, he caved in and moved to Thomasville to be with all of us. I moved out of John's house to live with Mother and Daddy in an apartment. Mother got a job working at a restaurant for about a year and actually never got paid a dime—there was always some reason that the owner couldn't come up with her pay. The only saving grace was that she brought dinner home from there, so at least we had some food on the table.

I was in 8th grade when I went to work at Florida Markets supermarket bagging groceries for 38 cents/hour, and I worked 40 hours a week while attending high school. I gave Mother my entire check to buy us all some groceries, which usually consisted

Rosalyn and Cromer McDaniels

of flour, rice, fatback meat, sugar, salt, and pepper. With just about every meal, we had rice or some kind of biscuit, but that was really all we had. And you never threw anything away. Ever. We lived in an apartment that cost $12.00/week, so the $20.00/week I was making at the supermarket didn't stretch very far. School wasn't all that important to me; in working 40 hours a week, I never really had time to study, play sports, or make many friends. For a while, Mother wasn't working, and neither was Daddy, so if I hadn't been working, we wouldn't have had money to eat.

I was growing up so fast. When I was a junior in high school, John helped me buy my first car for $550—a 1964 Ford Galaxy. My payments were $30.00/month and I felt on top of the world. All the work I had been putting in was finally paying off. I'd only had the car for about four months, and one day, I was driving along the main street in Thomasville when a beautiful girl caught my attention. (I always was a sucker for a pretty face!) As I turned my head to look at her, the driver in front of me decided to take a quick left-hand turn and just stopped... and that was the end of that car. Throughout the rest of my high school years, I had to hitch rides everywhere I went until I saved up enough money to get another car. My senior year, I bought a brand new 1966 Mercury Comet with a payment of $88/month. At that time, I was working at Johnsontown Supermarket making $56/week.

In 1967, I graduated from Thomasville High School and I was pretty proud of myself; I was the first McDaniels to do it. The night I graduated, I told Mother that I wanted to go to a tech school in Florida because I saw that computers were all the rage and I wanted to learn all about them. Tuition was going to be $800-900/year, plus I had to have money to get down there and find a place to stay. My mother told me, "Son, we can't do it. There's just no money to do this."

Knowing I couldn't go to tech school, reality set in, and I really only had two choices: either go to the Air Force for four years or get drafted into the Army for two. I knew that I didn't want to go to Vietnam because things were really heating up with that war, so I made another big decision: I joined the Air Force.

TAKING SHORTCUTS

Not long after graduation, I got the letter stating I had to report to Charlotte, NC on August 17, 1967, and would be officially signed into the Air Force.

The same day I was signed in, they flew me to Lackland Air Force Base in San Antonio, TX, home of the Alamo. Just like that, another chapter of life was about to begin. I think I only saw my daddy tear up one time in his life, and that was the day I left for service; they were tears of pride.

I had two buddies who were supposed to join the Air Force with me: George and Curtis. None of us had money for college— we were just too poor. We were all supposed to report to Charlotte to be sworn in together; we were going in on the "buddy plan," or so I thought. As it turned out, I was the only one who showed up that day, and I think that's a decision they might've regretted for the rest of their lives. Within 30 days, each of them were drafted by the Army.

George was sent to basic training, returned back home for ten days, then was shipped right off to Vietnam. He arrived there on November 25, 1967, the day before Thanksgiving, and also his birthday. He was sent into a tunnel which happened to be booby trapped, and sadly, he was killed that very day at only 19 years old.

Curtis was in the Army for about six months, then took a gamble and went AWOL to be with a girl he had fallen in love with. He left training and disappeared, hoping that no one would find him. It wasn't even a year later when he was arrested at home, sent back to the Army, and then shipped off to Vietnam. Curtis only had about three months left on his tour of duty when he and two other soldiers were driving a supply truck and ran over a landmine. One of the men in the truck was killed instantly, and Curtis' leg was blown to pieces, eventually amputated, and his arm was mangled from the shrapnel. He ended up living his life as a disabled veteran.

I still wonder how their lives might be different today if they had just shown up with me in Charlotte that day. They made the decision to roll the dice for less time in the military, but it wasn't a good decision. It wasn't a safe decision. It was a gamble. Sometimes taking risks is a good thing, but you have to go back to those consequences; losing a leg or your life are some pretty big ones. There are a lot of times you can make a decision to take a shortcut and follow the quicker or easier path based on what feels good in the moment, rather than basing your decision on what will set you up to be the most successful in the long run. That has been a huge lesson for me: taking shortcuts in life will often run you right into uncharted territory, causing you to wish you had just followed the route that was more certain.

As for me, I headed into the Air Force quite willingly, expecting to serve the standard four-year term. I flew from Charlotte to Dallas, then on to San Antonio through the most unforgettable storm I had ever seen. As I was watching lightning bounce off the wings of the plane, I thought I had made the worst decision of my life. I was sure I was going to die that night, but by the grace of God, I arrived at Lackland around 5 am, and they woke us up three hours later. I remember thinking, "What have I gotten myself into?"

They treated us like crap, of course, and they scared the daylight out of us. I went through basic training pretty easily, and before long, I was finding my way. I had more clothes than I'd ever had in my life: five dress uniforms, five pairs of khakis, plenty of underwear, t-shirts, socks, shoes, boots, hats, and three squares a day! Looking back, I have so much appreciation for my time

As a USAF Airman

in the military. It taught me discipline in a whole new way—discipline I needed in order to be successful. When I put that uniform on, I thought, "This is actually pretty nice!" My shoes were polished, my uniform was pressed neatly… already, I had come a long way from where I started.

Being in the service was probably the easiest job I ever had because I only had to work from 8 to 4 and got 30 days of paid vacation. The pay wasn't a whole lot, but the discipline I learned helped me set the standard that I live by to this very day.

REINVENTING YOURSELF

"It isn't the strongest species which survives, neither the most intelligent, but rather that which adapts best to change."

—*Charles Darwin*

There have been times in my life that required me to intentionally reinvent myself, and I think joining the Air Force was the first time I really did it. There are some people in life who possess an extraordinary capacity to conquer adversity and who rarely lose their patience. Developing this kind of resilience is essential when it comes to reinventing yourself. Our mental software is made up of our experiences, but that doesn't mean you have to surrender to those experiences and live your life based on what you've gone through. Your convictions are a choice. What you believe you can achieve in life is a choice you make every day when you wake up. And it really is everything.

Reinventing yourself requires you to let go of whatever identity you've created from your previous life experiences and allow the possibility that your life can take a new turn if you really want it to. You've got to pay close attention, but you can feel it—those times when life feels stagnant or even worse, comes crumbling down around you. If the decisions you've made haven't gotten you to where you want to be, then it may be time to reinvent yourself. The key is to focus on what you want, not on your shortcomings.

Is it scary? Absolutely. I'd be lying if I said I wasn't scared to leave my family behind and move to North Carolina at only 15 years old, or to board a plane whisking me off to the Air Force for the next four years of my life with no idea what to expect. But how much scarier can it be than staying where you are, day after day, for the rest of your life, feeling unfulfilled, unsatisfied, and unsuccessful? That's just too many "uns!"

I've learned that when opportunity knocks, you have to be ready to open that door and jump right through it without hesitation, *especially* when it's scary. There's a quote by Anthony De Mello that says, "Those that think too much before stepping forward spend their lives on one leg." I love that.

Too often, life is full of "you shouldn't" or "you ought to"—be careful of these. And be mindful when you hear them whispering in your ear. They can land you in a hum-drum life faster than you can go from zero to sixty in a Porsche 911 Turbo. When you're reinventing yourself, you're not becoming someone else so much as you're unbecoming the person you no longer want to be. It all goes back to those choices and decisions.

The most important thing to remember in making new decisions is to change your state of mind. You can do this by changing who you hang around with, changing your daily routine, and changing your environment. When I left Floyds and headed for Thomasville, I was starting the process of reinventing myself without even realizing it. When I made that one decision, God began opening more doors. Reality is whatever you make it. You get to choose.

If you're not willing to shift gears, you'll be stuck in park.

CAPITALIZING ON A HOT COMMODITY

In business, you've got to go after something that people value; the more value something has, the more demand there is for it, which drives up the premium. This was a lesson I learned in the Air Force personnel department. At the time, the Air Force implemented a deal that if you reenlisted after serving two and a half years, they would pay you a bonus as if you had stayed in for the full four-year term. My job was to interview every airman and explain the benefits they'd receive if they reenlisted; a $10,000 check was the carrot at the end of the stick.

Naturally, each person I interviewed would ask, "Bill, what are you going to do? Are you staying in?" I would respond with, "Let me ask you a couple of questions: When's the last time you took your wife to dinner? When's the last time you went out and bought her a new dress? I don't have any control over whether or not you can pay your bills, but you have a choice: stay right where you are financially, or receive a $10,000 check from me, tax-free." Now, you have to remember that back then, most folks had never even seen $10,000, let alone all in one check. Then I would ask them, "What is the first thing you would do with that money if you decide to reenlist?", and 99% of them would say, "I'd buy a car." It didn't take long to see that cars were a very hot commodity, and that's where it all began. I knew there was something to the car business because everybody wanted one! I thought, "Holy cow! There's an opportunity here!" and the wheels started turning.

THE POWER OF A HANDSHAKE

One day, I went to the local Chevrolet dealership, traded in my '69 Volkswagen, and bought myself a '70 Chevy Malibu. That's where I met Jim Stanley and told him about my job in the Air

Force; he quickly introduced me to Mr. Mathis, who owned that dealership. I shared with him that I was an airman at Shepherd Air Force Base working in career motivation, and that my job was to allocate bonus money and reenlist airmen after they had served 30 months in the military. My idea was that I would refer everyone who agreed to reenlist to Mr. Mathis, and in return, he would pay me $100 for each sale.

The way I saw it, we could sell at least ten cars a month, but I sweetened the deal even more by allowing every one of those airmen to drive the car the day before they got their $10,000 bonus. Mr. Mathis would deliver the car, and I would bring him the money about three weeks later when the actual check was received. And all of this was done on a handshake. Can you imagine putting that level of trust in someone? I can tell you that I never once let him down, because back then, your word and your handshake were all you had. He knew we had a good thing going, and I knew it too. I estimated that after three and a half more years in the service, I could either be making $241/month as a sergeant or making $1000/month selling cars. My decision was made!

DEPRECIATION

Being in the military gave me time to mature and really think about what I was going to do with my career, and I'm very grateful for the time that I served and the many valuable lessons I learned. One of the biggest lessons that stands out is how quickly a hot commodity can turn into a nonentity if the value becomes unappreciated or unneeded. This goes for products and people alike.

Here's my theory on depreciation: I believe you have about 25 years—from about age 25 until you're about 50—to really make something of yourself. You're very attractive to businesses to hire you if you're a go-getter and you're willing to put in the time and effort to be successful. Once you get past the age of 50, it's a little like trying to find someone to marry who doesn't have any baggage at that age. Hard to find! I recognized this concept while I was in the Air Force. I witnessed some people who were very career-minded get kicked out after serving for many years, and that was one of the main reasons I chose not to reenlist.

This very scenario happened to Sergeant Sheppard, who had completed two tours in Vietnam and served loyally for almost 20 years. When he went to get his orders for the third tour, he was rejected and disqualified to remain in the Air Force because he didn't pass his annual physical. He had given over 19 years of service and never received a dime of retirement money—not even a small severance as a thank you. He only had six more months left to serve. I can still see the look on his face when he told me his story. I remember thinking, "If that could happen to a Sergeant with 19 years of service, it could certainly happen to a young buck like me." I was 20 years old when I watched that happen, and I promised myself that that would not be my story.

Learning from others' experiences and making decisions based on what you've seen is a powerful tool. When you see something you don't want for yourself, make a mental note and choose another path.

CHAPTER 3

FIRSTS

Heading into my 20s, I was like every other guy—going out and chasing girls every weekend and spending my money just about as fast as I made it. I think I loved the chase even more than I did the catching, but I was doing just fine when it came to dating; the biggest problem was, I was always broke! I was only making $41.00 every two weeks, and my gas bill was about $10.00 a month. The first weekend after getting paid, I'd quickly find myself down to about $10.00 left in my pocket, so if you were with me and you wanted to go out, you had to pay! My buddy and I worked in the building where all the girls who were fresh out of basic training would come every Friday night, and they couldn't wait to go out; so, lucky for us, the pickins' were pretty easy.

After a while, I decided it was probably time to find a good girl and settle down, and that's what I did. She worked in personnel with me, and she was the fastest typist I had ever seen. From a small town in Georgia, she didn't grow up with much more than I did, and she enlisted in the Air Force to escape her hometown and make something more of her life—we had that dream in common. One day, I needed some typing done for a report, so I asked her if she'd help me out. I told her that if she could type what I needed, I'd take her to dinner. Needless to say, she finished it in no time, handed me the report, then asked with a grin what time I'd be picking her up.

We began seeing each other, and not even a year later, on September 13, 1969, I married Darlene Bunn. Darlene was the epitome of a "good girl." She was genuinely kind, just like my mother was, and I trusted her fully. There's a certain amount of worry that you don't have to think about when you find someone who is forthcoming and trustworthy, and I really value that in any relationship. We set up house and stayed in the Air Force until we were discharged. We were just getting on our feet and were able to get an apartment with our two incomes and start our life together. Life was good, and we were happy.

Both of us got out of the Air Force on February 16, 1971, and we moved back to Thomasville. I had served only three and a half of my four years because Vietnam was coming to an end, and they offered me an early out to go back to college on the GI Bill. I took that deal and went to Davidson County Community College in Lexington, NC and graduated with my associates degree in 1973—another "first" in the McDaniels family history books. But by far, the very best "first" was the birth of the light of our life, Tracey.

Talk about unforgettable moments... Tracey was such a beautiful baby, absolutely precious. Minutes after she was born, I remember promising her that on her 16th birthday, I'd buy her the most perfect gift: a new car. She was everything to me and still is—a total "daddy's girl." She was quite the performer, always singing and dancing... she really didn't have a shy bone in her body. She was vibrant and full of energy. I remember we used to sing Neil Sedaka's song "Breaking Up is Hard to Do," and she knew every single word.

"Ambition is a dream with a V-8 engine."
—Elvis Presley

When Tracey was growing up, I was working on all eight cylinders because I wanted her to have the best life possible; but as I look back on things now, I wish I would've better understood the importance of spending quality time with her because that's one thing you can't get back—time.

The car business can really take its toll on a family, and back then, it consumed me. My late twenties and early thirties were

Bill, Darlene, and Tracey

filled with selling cars, building houses, and building a family; most of the time, it was probably in that order. I was on the road to success, and I managed to save up enough money to buy my first home for $24,000—a brand new 1600 square foot brick house not even 1/2 mile from where Mother and Daddy lived. It had a nice kitchen, a real fireplace, three bedrooms, and two bathrooms. Daddy thought it was the nicest home he had ever seen, and it probably was.

By this time, Daddy was working at Thomasville Veneer Factory. I had only been home from the military for a few short years when Daddy was diagnosed with cancer. It was the day after Thanksgiving, 1973. He was given anywhere from 1-5 years to live

With Tracey

and he started chemo. He was in so much pain because the cancer traveled quickly to the lymph nodes. The crazy thing about it was, I had been trying to get him on Medicare and disability for over two years because he had been sick prior to receiving the cancer diagnosis; when I say, "trying," I mean going back and forth with the government on a regular basis. It was a battle.

On January 28th, 1974, at only 59 years old, Daddy had a stroke and was placed on life support. I was at work when the hospital called and told me he had passed. Before I could even take a breath, I received another call. It was the Social Security office telling me they had finally approved Daddy for disability. I was 29 years old when he died on February 11th at 4:07 pm. Experiencing the devastating and life-threatening effects of cancer so intimately is what sparked my biggest mission in life today—to raise as much money for cancer research and prevention as I can in this lifetime. Rest in peace, Daddy.

After receiving my associates degree, I attended the University of North Carolina-Greensboro to get my bachelor's degree, and I went to work in High Point, NC for Van York Pontiac Honda. Those days were especially tough on my family. Most days, I wouldn't walk through the front door until somewhere around 9 pm. Darlene was working full-time at a fabric company, and I'm sure she felt like she was taking care of Tracey all by herself, but at the time, I was chasing that "streetcar named desire," and I was determined to achieve.

I was spending almost as much money on my college books as I was getting paid from the GI Bill, so I was grinding from week to week, living from paycheck to paycheck… and I stopped and asked myself, "What the heck am I doing?" I was really going to school blind, not having a clue what I wanted to do at the end of it. I had always wanted to go to college and thought that having a degree was what mattered the most to get ahead in life. I was only 32 hours short of getting my bachelor's degree when I closed the hood on going to school; and to be honest, I'm ok with that. College was one of the few things in life that I ever gave up on, but it wasn't for lack of interest or ambition. Money was tight, we now had a house payment and a baby, and driving back and forth to college just didn't make much sense.

I also realized that the business classes I was taking in school didn't mean a thing to me. If I had a degree, perhaps the most money I could make back then was about $7,500 a year. How were these classes going to affect my car sales business and everything I was now pouring into it? Looking back, if I had skipped college altogether and concentrated on nothing but selling cars from the get-go, I probably could've doubled what I was making. What I knew in my soul was that I really loved meeting people. That was my true passion. So, I made the decision right then and there; that was a defining moment and another major turning point in my life.

SIGNING ON THE DOTTED LINE

Right about the time I made the decision to pursue my dreams in the car business, I got my first credit card—an American Express with a $5,000 line of credit. That was a lot of money back then! All I had to do was sign the card, but then I had to decide what to do with all that money. My vision was to own a dealership of my own one day, which started with "looking the part," so I maxed out the card with $5,000 worth of clothes. Not just any clothes—suits. I committed to two things: working harder than anyone else and being the best-dressed guy in town. You know how the saying goes: "You never get a second chance to make a first impression," and first impressions—especially in the car business—can make or break your career.

DETAILING

There's nothing sexier than sliding into the driver's seat of a freshly detailed car. The leather shines, the rims sparkle, and I truly believe the car drives better. And you feel better driving it! That's exactly how I felt when I slid into one of my new suits: polished, confident, and fierce.

Feeling freshly detailed, I met with Mr. York, told him I was done with school, and that I was going to focus solely on selling cars. I remember him congratulating me on my decision; in my first year at York Pontiac Honda, I made $24,000—triple what an entry-level business job would've gotten me. From that point on, I blew everybody away at selling cars at that dealership. A couple of the salespeople even tried to get me fired because I was selling so many cars; they insisted I was stealing their customers. They were like crabs in a bucket—when one tries to get out, the others are right there pulling it back down.

One day, four of the salespeople met with Mr. York and said, "Bill is stealing our customers and it's not right." Mr. York said, "Well, let's get Bill in here right now and I'll just fire him. But before I do, how about writing down the names of the customers that he's stolen from you." They all stood there for a minute, but nobody could write down a single name. They complained that I was staying at work after the dealership closed and collecting the names and telephone numbers of the people who stopped by in the evenings to browse around. And that's exactly what I was doing! It was a fantastic strategy! I had the whole lot to myself— the perfect opportunity to connect with people. The following day, I would come into work in the afternoon and call each and every one of them. It was working. I was selling more cars than all of the other salespeople. When Mr. York heard this, he told them, "I'm going to fire every one of you if you don't get your butts out there and start selling some cars. Maybe you should think about doing what Bill is doing."

I sold cars for Mr. York from May 1973 to December 1979. In my last year, I sold 234 cars and increased my annual income to $59,000, which was more than twice the amount the General Manager made. Was I competitive? You better believe I was. I was determined to be first.

There was one month when the whole dealership of 11 sales-people sold 71 cars, and I had sold 35 of them. I think that record still stands, even today, but who's counting? It didn't make me a very popular person to the rest of the team, but it didn't matter to me one bit. If there was a bonus announced, I was getting it, no doubt about it. That was really the time that my drive to be successful rose to a whole new level.

By the time I was 30 years old, I knew in order to get that first dealership of my own, I needed to get serious about saving money instead of spending it. I looked into buying into other dealerships at a 10% or 20% partnership, but all of the deals fell through for one reason or another. I needed more money. I had a family, a new house, a brand-new car, and I no longer had to worry about school; so, what was my next step? It didn't take me long to recognize that I needed to make some moves in order to make my mark.

BUILDING AN OPPORTUNITY

1973 marked another "first"; I built my first house. It all started with a torn-out page from a Better Homes and Garden magazine. I had seen a picture of a brick ranch house that sat on a lake, and I tore it out and put it up on my wall at work. I just loved that house. I looked at it every day. One of my customers had come in looking for a car, commented on the picture, and I told him confidently, "I'm going to build that house one day."

Two years later, that same guy came back into the dealership and the clipping was still pinned up on my wall. He asked, "Bill, did you ever build that house?" I shook my head no. He pressed a little further, "Are you going to build it?" and that just really pissed me off! So, I replied with conviction, "Yes, I am." I had already ordered the blueprints for it, so the very next day, I took them down to the savings and loan and I asked to borrow $50,000, having no idea if they'd give it to me or not. The following day, they called me and told me I had the loan! I thought, "Well, that wasn't so hard!"

I thought if I could build a house and flip it, then I could make up the difference to buy that 10-20% partnership. When I went home to tell Darlene that we were about to build a new house and the payments would be $325 more per month than what we were currently paying, she just about fell off her chair. But I had already figured out that if I sold just one more car per month, we'd be covered; I just had to work a little harder. I knew I could do better. I knew I could figure out how to be more successful, and the harder I worked, the more success was coming to me.

The fact that I would be spending even more time away from the family to build this house wasn't the best news. Darlene wanted me to be home every night for family dinner and to put Tracey to bed, and I didn't blame her. But here's the thing: I wanted more—for myself and for all of us. To Darlene, building that house meant taking a big risk, and risk wasn't something she was very comfortable with.

To me, all I could think about was the last house I lived in before I had moved to NC—that worn-down old schoolhouse with no running water, no bathroom, no nothing. I was so embarrassed at the lack of what we had; to be honest, there were a lot of times growing up when we were treated like straight trash.

I guess it was just pride that motivated me to decide that I would never again be thought of the way I had been as a child. There was no way I could ever go back to that. I was getting a small taste of success for the first time where I wasn't destitute and poor, and the more I created that separation, the more driven I became.

So, we broke ground on that house from Better Homes and Gardens, and it took me about a year to finish; it was my biggest accomplishment yet. It sat right on Oak Hollow Lake, and you could see the lake from the front of the house. It was beautiful. The problem was, the harder I worked, the more cars I sold, the more money I made, and the less time I had for my family.

When you're younger, you don't always consider how your decisions are going to affect the people you love. It's easy to overlook the signs that might be right in front of you—you just

The first house I built, 1975

don't want to see it. Then, as you get older and wiser, when you finally acknowledge those signs, you may discover that it's too late to undo the damage. You realize, "this just isn't going to work anymore."

We lived in that house for a few years before Darlene and I separated. I sold it in 1979 when our divorce was final and made $51,000 on it. Our marriage lasted nine years, and although Darlene and I didn't see eye to eye back then, I still love and respect her to this day. I'll always be grateful that marriage produced one of the most cherished people in my life, Tracey. I hope and believe that Tracey understands why I strived to accomplish so much in my life. I was escaping my past as much as I was building a future for my family. My relationship with Tracey is the best now that it has ever been, and she'll always be Daddy's little girl.

CHAPTER 4

DECISIONS AND CONSEQUENCES

I RE-MET MY SECOND WIFE, Pat, toward the end of 1979. We were high school friends, and she worked as a title clerk at the Honda dealership for about a year before my divorce with Darlene was final. We dated for almost a year before we got married on December 20, 1980. Pat's son, Rob, was 14 at the time, so in addition to Tracey, I now had a teenage son. Soon after we married, Pat got her real estate broker's license, I got my general contractor's license, and we started building houses under Bill McDaniels, Inc.

I would line up all the subcontractors and build the houses and she would manage the crews and pick out all the appliances and paint for the walls. Then she'd sell them. We made quite a good team. From 1981-1988, we built almost 25 houses, shooting for 3-4 houses per year. We lived in a new house, drove new cars, and it was a new experience not having to live paycheck to paycheck. I was working harder, but life was getting easier.

I saw a newspaper ad from Flow Motors in Winston-Salem looking for a new car manager, and I felt like my run at Van York was coming to a close. I didn't see myself going anywhere from where I was, and that bothered me because I had already cast my longer-term vision to own my own dealership. So, I applied at Flow Honda and was hired as the Sales Manager there in 1980. I made $139,000 dollars that year—$10,000 in one month, which was the first time I had ever accomplished that. I thought I had really made it. Confidence was in abundance, and life was moving right along.

In 1986, I bought into the Flow Acura dealership in Greensboro as a 25% partner. I helped it grow to the #1 Acura dealership in the state of North Carolina. I lived and breathed that business, and the Flow family became an extended part of my own. I was very close with them, or so I thought.

Between building houses and building a successful dealership, I worked nonstop, increasing my wealth more each year. Then, in 1988, I decided to do something I rarely did—take a vacation. To my complete surprise, when I returned from that vacation, Mr. Flow called me into my office and, out of nowhere, suggested that we sever our partnership. I couldn't figure out what was happening. I had no idea where this was coming from because I was performing at the top of my game. But the truth is, it didn't matter why. I was so disheartened and angered; without asking a single question, I simply said, "Okay."

I later found out that another employee told him I was spending too much time building houses, and apparently, he didn't like that. What bothered me the most was that he didn't even take the time to have a conversation with me about it; he had already made his decision. At the time, Rob was also working there in the parts department while he was home from Georgia Tech for the summer; so not only did I walk away, but I marched back to the parts department and said, "Rob, I just got fired, and that means you're fired, too." Although it was a big blow, it was also the wake-up call I needed to move on to bigger and better things. I wasn't about to let this keep me down.

LET'S MAKE A DEAL

In 1989, I moved to Columbia, SC and bought into the Century Acura dealership as a 30% partner with the Mims organization. From 1989-1992, I was living in a hotel and had gone right back to living from paycheck to paycheck. At the time, Century was without a doubt the nicest automobile facility in South Carolina, and maybe even the entire East Coast. It was also losing money faster than you could blink an eye. Acura had called me up to inform me that Frank Mims was looking for some help to turn his business around. The dealership had lost $625,000 in its first four months, and business was just getting worse.

When I met with Frank, I told him that I could help him, but it would require him to give me the autonomy to do what I needed to do to turn the dealership around. He agreed, and within the first month under my leadership, I drastically cut the expenses and cleaned house by firing 22 of the 23 employees there. The truth is, there was very little structure there and even less of a commitment to sell cars. Also, within that first month, I took the dealership from a $125,000 deficit to a $4,200 profit. I grant you, a $4,200 gain may not sound like a whole lot, but I was very proud to have saved a $125,000/month loser. From there, I never looked back.

Frank and I had an agreement that within two years, if I hadn't made enough money on my own, he would sell me the rest of the stock he owned at a predetermined price and help me with the financing to take it over. But I knew in my heart that in those two years, I could make enough money to completely buy him out. And that was my plan. It was a handshake deal, but I trusted him.

The first year, we were profitable and doing quite well. But one thing about the car business is that you never know what can happen to cause a lull in the market. In September of 1989, Hurricane Hugo hit the East Coast, which took out the electricity for an entire week, and the last thing on anyone's mind was venturing out to buy a new car. By December of that year, our profit had diminished to zero. The following year, The Gulf War took its toll on the economy, and we were still operating on a very small amount of profit. Once the soldiers came back home from the war, things began to turn around.

A week before we were to finalize the plans for me to take over the dealership, Frank called me to postpone our meeting because his banker, attorney, and CPA weren't available to meet—it was tax season and things were just busy. I wasn't fazed because I fully expected Frank to make good on our deal. Two days later, at only 55 years old, Frank died. After about a week, I met with his wife, Mary Louise, who was accompanied by her attorney and several others. She said she would honor my agreement with Frank about purchasing the balance of the stock for Century Acura, but there was a caveat: I had to pull everything together in only 30 days. Just getting approved to become a dealer in South Carolina took 2-3 months, and I didn't have a floor plan line from the bank, so we both knew the 30-day window was impossible.

For several months, it was business as usual. Then, on September 5, 1991, I received two phone calls that would change my life forever. The first call came from American Honda Finance congratulating me on being approved as a dealer in the state of South Carolina and giving me a floor plan line of $750,000. Not even five minutes later came the second call. It was Mary Louise. She told me she had changed her mind about honoring the original agreement I'd made with Frank—she decided to keep 51% of the business and offered me 49% to be her partner.

She had made a complete and unexpected U-turn. To make matters worse, she only gave me a week to give an answer to her proposition. I was between a rock and a hard place. I remember sitting on my back porch agonizing over what to do. My vision was to own my own dealership outright, and the opportunity I had worked so hard for was about to slip through my fingers… or maybe not.

We were on track to clear about $300,000 for the year at Century, and I had poured everything I had into turning that dealership around. I didn't want to leave, but I had also told myself that Frank would be the last partner I'd ever have in this business.

During that week, I estimated that I had invested close to $150K into that dealership, so if I walked away from the deal, that would be my total loss. I also knew that, worst case scenario, if I left and went back to NC to work with another dealership as a partner, I could confidently make upwards of $300K/year. The clock was ticking, and it was time for me to make one of those big life decisions.

At the end of that week, with all my confidence, I walked into Mary Louise's attorney's office alone and was surprised to be greeted by an entourage of her attorneys, bankers, and CPAs. She came fully loaded, ready to seal the deal. But I had another plan. I walked into the room, calmly laid my keys down on the desk, looked into her eyes and said, "I'm not interested in partnering."

At that moment, the room was so still, you could hear a pin drop. I had a proposition of my own. I said, "I reject your deal, and here's what I'm going to offer to you: I'll reduce the price to take over the franchise as the sole owner, and the rent will be reduced by $3,000/month." As she began to cry, I excused myself from the room and said, "You have ten minutes to make a decision." When the ten minutes had passed, I walked back into the room and she begged me to reconsider. Of course, I declined.

You see, the hard truth was she knew good and well that if I left, the rest of the employees would follow me back to NC, and the doors to Century Acura would be closed in no time. I asked her, "What did your legal team advise you to do?" She replied quietly, "They told me to sell it." Needless to say, on October 2, 1991, I became the full owner of that Acura dealership, and Century Acura became McDaniels Acura—the first of many McDaniels dealerships to would follow. That moment… stepping right into the vision I had been holding for so many years was probably one of the most pivotal moments of my life, and it paved the way for my career that has made building the McDaniels Automotive Group a truly unforgettable ride.

KEEPING IT IN THE FAMILY

As the proud, full owner of my first dealership, I wanted my family that I had worked so hard for to be a part of this business. When Rob graduated with a degree in engineering from Georgia Tech in 1990, I gave him the option of finding a job in his field or coming to Columbia to work with me. Thankfully, he came on board and started selling cars, but it didn't take long for him to realize that Sales wasn't his cup of tea. He became Chief Operating Officer, which was the perfect role for him, and the one he continues to hold with McDaniels Automotive Group today.

The Acura dealership in Columbia was thriving, and I was focused on saving up for my next dealership. On April 1, 1999, I bought my second Acura dealership in Charleston, SC; on Jan-

NASCAR driving experience at Charlotte Motor Speedway
with my son, Rob

uary 1, 2000, I opened the McDaniels Porsche dealership in Columbia. In 2003, I broke ground on the Audi franchise, one in Charleston and one in Columbia. Shortly after, Tracey came to work with Rob and me in Charleston, and it was so wonderful to have my family along for the ride. I was opening dealerships bumper-to-bumper, which inevitably took its toll on my marriage with Pat. During all this business building, Pat was spending a lot of time back in Thomasville because we were building another house there for her family. We were seeing each other less and less and were growing further apart.

Pat and I divorced on August 16, 2006, which was truly the best thing for both of us, and I wish her the very best in life. I lived and learned through two divorces, and I can't help but look back and feel like, in a way, I failed. Sometimes I think, "I should've been able to fix that," and at the same time, I was just doing the best I knew how. Despite our marriage having its share of fender-benders, I wouldn't trade it for anything, because out of it came the best son I could ever ask for.

After the divorce, I met with Rob and expressed the love I have for him—I had divorced his mother but I could never divorce him. I wanted him to know that he and his wife, Quinn, and my grandson Julian would always be part of my family. When Rob was 41, I legally adopted him; for 30 years, he has supported me and the McDaniels family business immensely, and he means the world to me.

CHAPTER 5

FINDING MY BALANCE

AFTER TWO MARRIAGES and two divorces, I can't say that I'm an expert on relationships, but I've certainly gained some valuable wisdom from my experiences. Perhaps more than anything, I've learned that relationships are like tires—you have to keep them balanced in order to experience the smoothest ride.

As you drive a car over time, the tires will naturally wear down and lose their traction, and eventually, the wear and tear throw the balance of the car completely out of whack, causing a wobbly, shaky, uncomfortable ride. In order to get the best performance and the most miles out of your car (and your relationships), there are certain adjustments you have to make along the way to continually restore the balance. Though there are many areas in life that need to be kept in balance, I believe there are three that are the foundation for a successful relationship: health, family, and faith.

On November 2, 2004, I was introduced to a woman who would prove to be the person to teach me more about balance than anyone else: Suzanne Pucci. When Suzanne and I first met, we were both married and living in Charleston, and I was in the process of building my Audi dealership there. Suzanne had asked a mutual friend where she should go to buy a new car, and he put her in touch with me. I called her immediately and she bought her car. Within about 18 months, we had both moved to Columbia, and she brought her car into the dealership for service. Sometime later, we had a chance meeting at Garibaldi's; she was having dinner with some business associates, and I was there having dinner with a friend. She approached me to tell me what a great experience she had with the dealership and complimented the people who took such good care of her and her car. She also shared that she had been invited to play in my annual golf tournament that was scheduled for that same week.

At the golf outing, I greeted her and we chatted about her successful business with Stanley Steemer. I had some carpets at my dealerships in both Columbia and Charleston that needed to be cleaned, so I asked if we could meet to discuss an estimate on the carpet cleaning. The following week, she came into the dealership in Columbia to meet with me, and then drove to the dealership in Charleston the following day. When the crew came to do the job in Charleston later that week, she accompanied them. By this time, I couldn't help but acknowledge our attraction and wasn't about to let another opportunity pass to ask her out on a date. Unfortunately, she had already made plans to go to a concert that night, which I boldly asked her to blow off so I could take her to dinner instead. She said no, but the following night, April 30, 2006, she said yes to dinner and we began seeing each other. Both of our divorces were finalized later that year, and we eventually moved in together; just as with any new relationship, we were trying to find our balance.

RECHARGING MY BATTERY

The first area that was out of balance was the difference in how Suzanne and I approached our health. Suzanne was always focused on fitness and her physical health—eating healthy, exercising regularly, and just generally taking good care of herself. I, on the other hand, was overweight and had a middle-aged potbelly from eating carelessly. Suzanne was a huge influence on my decision to start taking better care of my health, always encouraging and supporting me. To be honest, I thought I was pretty invincible, but that all shattered on May 31, 2015, when I suffered a heart attack that shifted my entire perspective on the importance of being healthy. Before the heart attack, because of her example, I had already begun making small strides to change my diet and exercise habits; if it weren't for her influence, I'm not sure I would be alive to be writing about it today.

With relationships, I believe it helps to have someone who thinks the way you think, who can support you in the goals you're trying to achieve. It's not that you can't do it on your own, but it's a whole lot easier when you're doing it together. You need people in your life to support you and hold you accountable, and she does that for me in so many ways. Just as you have the choice to sleep in later and veg out on the couch at the end of the day, you also have the choice to set an intention to tackle each day by making healthier choices. After my heart attack, I began waking up at 5:30 every morning. Before anything else, I have a cup of hot tea and some yogurt and I read my daily Bible passage. Most days, I run close to three miles, too. Why? Because it sets the tone for the entire day. If you don't have your health, it makes it very difficult to live your life at the highest level.

STAYING IN MINT CONDITION

Another reason for maintaining a healthy body is that appearance matters! Some people surrender to the idea that as you get older, it's ok to let yourself go—you've paid your dues, you've earned the right to be unhealthy and tired. I couldn't disagree more. There's always time to make some small changes in your life and continue to improve yourself; you just have to make the decision to get off your butt and do something about it! Blinking your eyes like "I Dream of Jeannie" or clicking your heels like Dorothy in "The Wizard of Oz" just isn't going to cut it. You have to make the decision to get into action. The thing about life is we don't know how much time we're given—tomorrow isn't promised—which is all the more reason to get focused. I believe that 100 percent.

STEERING IN THE SAME DIRECTION

Many relationships suffer due to a lack or breakdown of trust, and I believe that trust is cultivated through the development of integrity. You can be trusted because you have a good reputation, but reputation is based on what others think or believe about you. Integrity, on the other hand, is what you know or believe about yourself; when you live in alignment with your integrity, others are able to trust you based on first-hand experience.

Integrity is shaped by our most valuable life lessons, the lessons that impact our deepest issues of honesty and motivation. Integrity is built through humble introspection, not self-righteous declaration. When you can look in that rearview mirror and learn from your past mistakes, you have the opportunity to look deep inside your heart and question how you would do things differently if you had it to do all over again. Integrity is shaped by how you respond and bounce back from the toughest times in life. It's who we really are when no one's watching.

Because of the importance Suzanne and I place on living in integrity, we are able to trust each other emphatically, and we value that trust more than anything. When you live with integrity, you eliminate the other person's need to doubt your true character; you know who they are, what they stand for, and how they will show up in any given situation. So, how do you develop it? Simple. Make sure your actions match up with your words in all areas of life. Honesty and trust are central to integrity, and these are probably the most important qualities to have in your relationships.

"Values are like fingerprints. Nobody's are the same, but you leave them all over everything you do."
—*Elvis Presley*

A person who has integrity lives their values in their relationships, so you need to know what those values are for your spouse or life partner and ensure they're in balance with your own. For instance, I mentioned that my commitment to being healthy is one of my top values, but it wasn't always that way. I paid attention to how much Suzanne valued her health, and I wanted to adopt that value for myself—not just because it was good for me physically, but because it was a value that we could hold as a couple and work on together. But health isn't just about taking care of the body, it's about taking care of the mind and the spirit, too. You have to want to continually improve yourself in all three areas to maintain that balance.

RIDING HIGH

Taking care of our spiritual health is another of our shared values that has improved our lives and our relationship tremendously. In creating balance in your life, I believe, first and foremost, you have to have a relationship with God at the center. No two people are ever going to have all the same opinions or agree on every little thing, but if you can find someone who thinks the way you do on most things and who wants to grow in their spirituality, you've got the main ingredients for a successful relationship.

Having grown up dusting church pews in a Pentecostal Holiness church as a child, my idea of spirituality couldn't have been more different from Suzanne's, who grew up in the Catholic faith. As our relationship progressed, although we were connecting in many other areas, this was one we hadn't figured out until a couple years ago when we found our way to GraceLife Church in Columbia.

Early in our relationship, we went to Catholic mass, but it wasn't the right fit. I think Suzanne and I were looking for a church that felt like home for both of us. In 2015, Suzanne noticed a vacant building close to our house, and she told me she was thinking about buying it. Before we knew it, there was a sold sign on it, and they built GraceLife Church.

Suzanne was really intrigued and decided to attend service there one Sunday. She was quite surprised to be in a non-denominational church amongst a very diverse congregation with a live band that was rocking out! She loved it. Eventually, when I decided to go with her, I was just as surprised at how connected I felt when I walked through those doors. We've been attending GraceLife for over a year now, and finding that balance through our faith has helped us continue to grow in countless ways to become the people we want to be for each other.

GraceLife Church

Since I was a young boy, I've always known that God had big plans for my life. I think it's easy to get wrapped up in your day-to-day routine and lose sight of the fact that we are all here for a unique purpose. One thing is sure: the longer I live, the clearer I am that God's purpose for me is so much bigger than I could've ever imagined for myself; that's why I wake up every morning looking forward to being here yet another day.

Suzanne and I try to read the Bible every night. We don't shove our beliefs down people's throats, and at the same time, we want to stand for our values and the ideals that are important for the betterment of ourselves and for the world around us. We want to be part of helping people and creating an image and standard that we can get things done because we're part of a community that gives back. And the beautiful thing is, we've found so many people who want to get on that wagon and help us on our journey of giving back. It feels so good to be a blessing to others; that's why I do what I do. I really think that is the only reason that we are here. It's not about getting a pat on the back, it's about giving your daily gratitude and knowing that you're helping others in some positive way.

It's easy to forget that the life we live on Earth is very short. Life blows past us like blur, but through Jesus Christ, we have been promised eternal life that is full of happiness. So, I believe that for the journey we are on here and now, we should be driving toward creating that happiness every second of every day and not wasting a single moment of it.

I believe there's a good reason that God refers to us as His children; it's because family is the greatest gift He can ever give us. Looking back on my life, I'm able to see how much of a challenge it was to find a healthy balance in building a successful business and being there for my family in a way that worked for everyone. In learning from many of the choices I've made, I've come to re-alize that building a close connection with family is what I value

With Suzanne on Air Force Two

most in my life, and Suzanne has been a beautiful example of this. It's very important to me to be with someone who values family like I do, and she calls her parents every day to check on them. She's close with her siblings, and she has embraced my family with open arms from the start.

> *"When people are free to do as they please, they usually imitate each other."*
>
> —*Eric Hoffer*

Suzanne has helped me to reinvent myself in a lot of ways. I credit her for how she has shown me to live a more abundant life by focusing on my health, my relationship with God, my relationship with my family, and on becoming a better person than I was the day before. There are bigger and better things that we both want to do in this lifetime, and growing as individuals enables us to grow closer together.

Oftentimes in relationships, there can be a battle for control over certain things or a desire to force someone to change. Neither one of us has control over the other; we don't want it. It's much better to have freedom and to give that back in return. And that's the beautiful part about it. I am still a work in progress, and I want to be the best person I can be every day, but I know that I'm never going to be perfect. If I strive to be a perfect human being… well, there really is no such thing. But by creating the balance through health, family, and faith, I've become a better person, a better partner, and a better Christian. Being well-balanced is one of the reasons for my success, but it hasn't been easy. I had to work at getting it that way and it required a lot of sacrifice. Suzanne has shown me that we can have it all. Her love has blessed my life in so many ways, and I can fly higher and farther with her beside me.

CHAPTER 6

CHOOSING YOUR RIDE

"The two most important days of your life are the day you are born and the day you find out why."

—*Mark Twain*

I WAS BORN FOR THE car business. The McDaniels Automotive Group has my DNA in it, and I've been extremely blessed to have my family share in my vision and be a part of it on a daily basis. One thing I learned early on is that if you don't have a vision, you're not in control of where you're going. Back in 1980, I was making about $135,000 a year, which was a lot of money then, but it wasn't enough to fuel my vision of owning multiple dealerships. That's when I decided to get my general contractor's license and start building and flipping houses.

I didn't realize it at the time, but when I pinned up that magazine clipping of my dream house, I had created a vision for how I wanted to live. When I imagined owning my first dealership and held onto that intention, it eventually happened. Having a vision with the things you want in life is an essential part of building success, but it takes more than just dreaming. When you have a big vision, you have to be willing to pay the price for it.

Successful people are able to determine what the most important things are in life and say no to the rest.

I've noticed that the most successful and respected people are able to do more and accomplish more, and one of the biggest reasons for that is they've learned the art of mastering self-control. They're able to determine what the most important things are in life and then say no to the rest. They have self-control over their attitudes when adversity hits, and they find a way to either work around it or power right through it and set their sights on the next thing. The harder you work on the things that are most important, the more you'll find yourself cruising through green lights along the way.

That's how you put yourself in a position to win. I've preached this concept to a lot of people—my salespeople, especially. The only reason a salesperson fails in this business is because they give up on it too soon. If they just stick around for five years, I guarantee they could make six figures. But too many people give up after they've have a bad month. I look back and wonder, "What if I had given up?"

In my first month selling cars, I only sold one. And the second month? Just one. As with any new endeavor, the first year is always the toughest. You have to accept that it's going to take some time to get acclimated and learn the ropes. Here's the formula to becoming a good car salesperson: in your first year, if you sell ten cars a month, you've sold 120 cars. In the second year, you'll probably get 20% of the first bunch back from the previous year, so you may pick up another 20 cars or so; now you're selling 140 cars per year. The third year, you pick up on the first two years, and by the time you reach the fourth year, the whole cycle of your original 120 is coming up again. Now you're selling about 240 cars. Then, in the fifth year, if you've continued to follow-up with your customers, you should be selling 250-275 cars, and you're easily making a six-figure income. More than anything, commitment and consistency are what contribute to becoming a successful salesperson.

RIDING THE WAVES

There's also a formula to having a 'good month' in the car business: you have to be positioned perfectly with the right mix of used cars, new cars, have no one out on vacation, and everyone is working together as a team. When those things are all in alignment, you feel like you're invincible and on top of the world. Then, you'll have those few months each year when sales are so scarce, you just want to pack it up and quit. There could be a snowstorm, a hurricane, or no reason at all… there are days when the customers just don't walk through the door.

Like many cyclical businesses, sales come in waves; you have to anticipate the ebb and flow because, as the old saying goes, "What goes up, must come down." The key is to keep replenishing your sales by generating your leads and making your follow up calls to your prospects, especially when business is slow. You have to keep working harder than everyone else.

When I was starting out in NC, I worked as hard as I could possibly work and prayed that someone was watching; as it turned out, someone was. The way I conducted myself, the way I dressed, and mostly the way I hustled was what opened the door to my vision of becoming a 30% partner at the first Acura dealership in Columbia. It wasn't by luck. It was by standing out from the rest of the crowd. I looked like I was on the road to success, and indeed, I was.

I remember the day I took that leap of faith, leaving life in Greensboro behind to move to Columbia—it was January 13th, 1989. I left to manage a dealership in Columbia that was struggling to survive, but I took a chance on turning it around. At the time when I needed business the most, we were hit with Hurricane Hugo, Desert Storm, and a recession. My marriage was declining. I had all the reasons in the world to wave the white flag of surrender, but I didn't. I couldn't. I had come too far working toward my vision, and refusing to give up changed everything. No excuses or setbacks were enough to force me to quit, and that dealership has opened so many more doors for me as time has gone by.

You don't have control of the waves; you just have to learn how anticipate them and then ride them.

There's always a rainy day in this business, but early on, I made the decision that no matter what's happening in the world, anything with the name McDaniels on it would be successful. You can't always see the storm coming, but when it comes, you just have to be ready; I've spent a lifetime preparing for those storms. I learned that even if I'm weathering a storm today, the sun's going to come up tomorrow. It may be cloudy, but rest assured, the sun is still shining behind those clouds—you've just got to look through them.

I work toward furthering my vision every single day. That's my main role in the McDaniels organization—to push it further—because the moment I quit growing is the moment people will start walking out the door. People want to work for a company that's profitable and continuing to grow, so I spend a lot of time keeping the momentum going. If you're not moving forward, you're going backward. And going backward is not an option.

TELL THEM WHAT YOU DO

Successful people can't wait to tell you what they do. This sounds simple enough, but you'd be surprised how many people sell cars and are ashamed of it. Sure, there are some salespeople who are afraid of being assigned the age-old persona of a "sleazy used car salesman," someone who will take advantage of you and sell you a lemon in a heartbeat. But I've spent my life's work on changing this perception by building a family business that values the highest level of honesty and integrity. When I'm out in the community introducing myself, I'm very proud to be a leader in the car industry, and I'm proud to tell people what I do.

Another thing is, the car industry is one of the few career opportunities where you can start selling without having two nickels in your pocket. You don't need to bring anything but yourself and a willingness to be of service to people. One of my passions is mentoring new salespeople because I remember how it was when

I was first starting out and how much I've learned about building lasting relationships over the years. There's an art to selling in a way that you're helping people to feel good about what they're buying, and one word that doesn't belong in the car business is the word "no." A good sales professional will come back and say, "I couldn't get exactly what you wanted done, but let me share what I *can* do for you." And 99% of the people will thank you and say, "Yes, I'll take that option." Why? Because you tried to help them! You didn't just say no and turn them away.

It's the little things that mean so much to the customer, like opening the doors for them and handing them the seat belt. If you go into a high-end hotel, they present you with the bill in a certain way, but very few people recognize and understand the art of those little nuances and what a difference they make to the customer. It's the little things that show you care about going above and beyond the norm. At the core, it's nothing more than common courtesy and being nice—that's all it really is. A McDaniels car may cost $100 more than what you can pay for it online, but the service you'll get over the life of that car is worth paying for. When you buy a car online, no one brings the car to you, shows you how to operate it, lets you drive it and test it out. You don't get to see it or touch it beforehand; there's no help on the other side of the sale. Having that relationship counts for a lot, especially when you're in a bind and you need something.

FEMALE HORSEPOWER

Developing solid people skills couldn't be more important in this business. To a large degree, I don't really think you can teach people skills; you either have a sales personality or you don't. You can train people on certain methods, but you can't give them the motivation, drive, and passion to make it work. And money isn't always the motivating factor. Some people just have a total lack of desire and want to take as many shortcuts as possible.

No matter what position you're in, the criteria is the same in becoming successful at what you do. You can see in a person's habits and performance if they have what it takes to be successful. In sales, you can't have an aggressive, overbearing approach—you have to have some patience in getting to know someone a little bit so you know what matters to them. And you know who's best at this? Women!

It may surprise you that 65% of all new cars are bought by women, and 89% of all car sales are heavily influenced by women. This business is starving for professional women. If more women knew how powerful and successful they could be in the car industry, we'd have a lot more of them on our sales floors, and I would welcome it.

Most men want to grab the keys, drive the car, and get the deal done as quickly as possible. With women, there's typically a more detailed rationale behind finding the car that's right for them—one that's big enough to haul four kids around to soccer practice, or one that has the highest safety rating. Simply driving the car with them isn't going to help you figure out what their needs and concerns are and what they want to accomplish. You have to have those people skills.

Another thing is, there is a high probability they won't buy the car the same day they first come in, so you have to learn as much as you can about them in order to help them down the road as best as you can. I want all my customers to have a comfortable buying experience and to leave happy, no matter what. As many cars as I've sold in over 30 years, there's still no greater feeling in the world than seeing the smile on someone's face who's found the right car and gets to drive it home. Creating an unforgettable buying experience has always been the passion behind what I do.

PURSUING YOUR PASSION

Getting up in the morning and loving what you do is a dream come true.

Another key factor in building a successful business is being able to recognize the people with talent. But as much talent as someone has, if they don't have the desire and passion behind what they're doing, they're probably not going to make it in sales. The same goes for life. You have to see your future with passion and zeal; if you don't, eventually, you're going to get tired of working so hard and realize that all you're doing is working for a paycheck. Passionate people have a vision that motivates them to live a full, successful life—not just financially, but in all areas. Passion propels business.

So, how do you find your passion? Well, I'll tell you… God leaves clues. If you don't know what your passion is, you just have to get better at looking around for the clues. What are you naturally good at? What do people tell you you're good at? If you don't know, ask the people who know you the best. What are some things you've always dreamed of doing but never had the guts to go after? You've got to feel a connection with what you do and why you're doing it or you'll find yourself in the wrong business.

It's easy to start a business; the hard part is keeping it. The average business lasts less than four years; mine has lasted for 31 so far, and it's stronger than ever. You have to keep that fire lit to go out and do it every day, and you do it by figuring out what your strengths are and where your passion lies. I make the most of every day that I'm given because I know that tomorrow isn't promised.

You should also pursue your passion in such a way that you're wide open to opportunities. The most important lessons in life can only be learned through the ups and downs, hills and valleys, successes and failures. You can reflect back on your life's toughest experiences and recognize the gifts that God put inside you, then be on a mission to unlock the doors to more opportunities, one failure at a time. If you're not sure which doors are the right ones, look for the ones that swing open easily. If you're tapped into your intuition, you'll be able to feel the perfect opportunity that has come in perfect timing; it will feel practically effortless. You also have to realize that once you've walked through the door, there will be setbacks. Naturally, you will make some choices that result in negative outcomes. But setbacks are temporary. The road to success is always under construction with roadblocks, potholes, dead ends, and detours; but those detours are often put there by God, who's always there, ready to help steer you back in the right direction.

PREPARING TO JUMP AND LIVING THE DREAM

"The future depends on what you do today."
—*Mahatma Gandhi*

Looking back, if there was someone who made a lasting impression on me, I'd have to say it was Jim Valvano, former Head Basketball Coach at NC State. Back in 1985, I was working for an auto group in Winston-Salem, and "Coach V" was the speaker at one of the dealership's events. He told a story about his parents who said to him, "Jimmy, if you keep your nose clean and stay outta trouble, you will be successful in life." And he said to us, "You know what? That was a lie. Because you can keep your nose clean and work all your life, but the only way you'll ever truly succeed is to be prepared for when an opportunity presents itself. When the window opens, you've got to jump through it without hesitation, because if you don't, that window will close just as fast as it opened." I'm a firm believer that in life, you may get only that one opportunity that can drastically change your life. You have to do everything you can to be ready for it.

> *"Your willingness to jump will open doors for you. Every jump will increase your wisdom and broaden your vision. The abundant life that God has in store for you will allow you to have unimagined riches; riches so overflowing that you'll have plenty—especially to share with others."*
> —Steve Harvey

Coach V also taught me that sometimes in an audience, you don't know who you're touching, but you better believe you're touching someone, if even just one. For that one person that you do touch, it could mean the difference of them living a life of mundane mediocrity or one of immeasurable success. So, when it comes to leadership, I try to always put my best foot forward so I can be a blessing to someone else.

As an entrepreneur, developer, and a person who's on the move, constantly trying to make things happen, there's nothing more critical than having a vision that directs your decisions. You have to be willing to take some big risks. You've got to be ready to step out of your comfort zone. God will bless your steps, as long as you're taking some. If you take a step, He'll take two; that's His promise.

> *"If you can dream it, you can achieve it."*
> —Walt Disney

The great Walt Disney couldn't have built the best theme park in the world if he didn't first have the dream to do it. The key word in his quote is "can." Having a dream is essential to building success, but it doesn't mean much if you don't put the hard work behind it.

In the book of James, the scripture reads, "Faith without works is dead. What does it profit, my brethren, if someone says he has faith but does not have works?" When God puts something in your imagination, you have to run with it. You can't let anyone else snuff out your fire, and you certainly shouldn't surround yourself with people who want to tell you all the reasons why your dream won't work. Making your dream come to life is 100% up to you.

Only ride with the people who walked with you.

Another critical success factor is who you choose to surround yourself with. It's so important to associate with the people in your life who are optimistic, intelligent, enthusiastic, pleasant, helpful, and who you admire. You have to create an environment of support and uplifting energy with people who promote positive thinking and innovative ideas—people who stretch you, challenge you, and most of all, believe in your dreams.

QUITTERS NEVER WIN, AND WINNERS NEVER QUIT

"I've quit a few times, but once you realize your problems are still there, you quit quitting."
—Raymond Ross

People are motivated to action when they see that something is possible, and I take pride in being one of those people. There have been so many opportunities for me to quit on my dream of building a family legacy, but quitters never win, and winners never quit. If you complain and dwell on what went wrong or went against your plan, you'll miss out on the next good thing. Think about rowing a boat in a river. If you're trying to paddle against the current (upstream), you'll spend so much of your effort fighting against the natural flow of the water. You'll become tired, frustrated, and defeated. But if you can learn from your bad decisions and find the lessons in them, you can simply turn the boat around and coast downstream with the flow.

PAYING THE PRICE

I've had my fair share of bad breaks, and I think if I'd had someone give me a few more good breaks along the way, what I could've accomplished would've been unbelievable. But I was willing to pay the price for my success, and I refused to quit. It reminds me of a song by James Brown, who sang "I don't want nobody givin' me nothin.' If you open up the door, I'll get it myself." I've had some doors that were closed, and they were meant to stay closed. I kept my head out of the sand, and when I got the opportunity, I was ready for it.

If you stay in this business, you can give your family a lot of things—a very good lifestyle—and that was a dream I could never give up on. There was too much at stake. I've paid a pretty good price to be in the car business in a lot of ways, but it has allowed me to give my family pretty much anything they wanted. When you're in the car business, your whole family is in it with you, like it or not. I feel so fortunate that my family wants to be in it with me, and "family" includes many of the people I've had the pleasure to work with.

One of those people is Raymond Ross, who I've known for 45 years and worked in the car business with for about half of those. I've always respected the way that Raymond maintained a healthy balance with his family, being in this business of long days and sometimes limited family time. Another thing I respect about him is something he said to me in a conversation once about quitting: "I've quit this job a few times, but once you realize your problems are still there, you quit quitting."

I couldn't agree more. Quitting doesn't make the problems that were there in the first place go away. You have to stay in it. This business still has one of the biggest turnover rates because people don't prepare with prospecting, and they take a break when times are good, which sets them up to fall hard when times are tough. They're not planning for the ups and downs, and they're not willing to ride the waves.

When people ask me if I'll ever sell the family business, not too long ago, I would've said, "I'd sell it! Almost everything is for sale." But now, I don't know that I'll ever sell it. I realize that all the money in the world couldn't bring me the happiness that I have coming to work every day to be with my family and employees (who I think of as family), and to be able to watch them grow and help them become successful. It's an honor to be a part of their lives.

CHAPTER 7

OPENING DOORS

"Life isn't a matter of milestones, but of moments."
                                        —*Rose Kennedy*

TIME IS OUR MOST valuable resource in life, and I wholeheartedly believe that the way you use your time directly affects the blessings that come into your life. In every moment, you have a choice in how you use it. Whether you waste it or make the most of it, once it passes, it's gone forever—you can never get it back. You can look back on what happened yesterday and look forward to what may happen tomorrow, but the true path to happiness is being present within each moment and living them to their fullest potential. For me, living life's moments to the fullest happens through giving, and there was no better teacher than my mother.

With all of the difficult times she experienced, Mother had every reason to wallow in her circumstances and haul around a mountain of negativity, but instead, she constantly found ways to give—to her children, to the church, and to everyone she met. She taught me the meaning of giving. If she had ten cents in her pocket, and she just met you and you needed it, she'd give it to you. No questions asked.

I grew up dirt poor; if someone was poorer than my family, it was pretty rare. And I almost couldn't believe that as hard as it was for us to survive and make ends meet, my mother still found a way to give. After she helped someone, I could always see the joy that it brought her. She would take two days to make a shirt or blouse for someone and she wouldn't charge them a thing. She loved to give. Like my mother, I give because I want to… because it feels good! I don't want or expect anything back. There are no strings attached to anything that I do.

My motive for giving is the feeling of satisfaction I get from helping a person or a cause, simply because I'm helping to make this planet a better place to live. You have to give in order to receive, and the more success you have, the more wealth you acquire, and

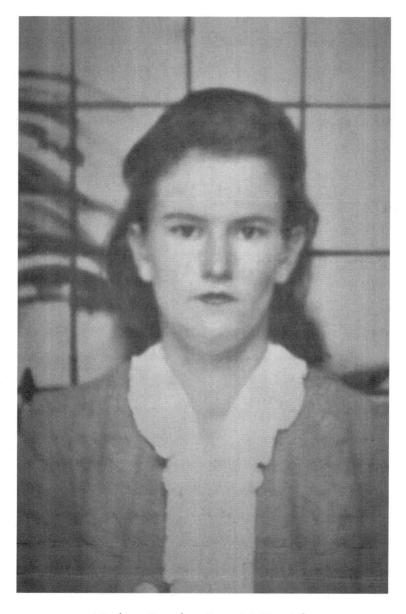

Mother, Rosalyn Russ McDaniels

the more you're able to give back. The best way to get through your own difficult times is to take the focus off of yourself and go help somebody else. I'm so thankful to my mother for being such a good example of this.

Another thing my mother taught me was that complaining about your circumstances does nothing to change them. It's one of the biggest time wasters there is. In fact, the more you focus on what's going wrong in your life, the more adversity and struggle you will draw into it. It's impossible to control every situation, but choosing to prepare for how you want to spend the moments in each day will result in more positive outcomes and a more satisfying life.

MY DRIVE TO GIVE

When it comes to money, so many people hold onto every last dollar they make and are afraid to let it go. But when you do that, you might as well be saying to God that you don't trust Him to bless you with more; what you're doing is worshipping money. On the other hand, some people believe that too much money is a bad thing. Of course, money can be the cause of broken relationships, business disputes, and so many other stressful situations. But it's all in how you look at it. If your drive is to possess money, to hold onto it as tightly as you can, it won't be long before it slips right through your fingers, causing you constant worry and fear. But if you accumulate it with the intention of doing something good in the world with it, you'll find that there's an endless stream of it. Your motivation behind acquiring money can absolutely affect whether it works *for* you or *against* you.

There's always enough and always more coming.

Giving is more than just an act to bring attention, significance, or pride to yourself. Giving is being of service to others, for no other reason than that's what God calls us to do. The Bible tells us things like, "Love thy neighbor," and, "To whom much is given, much is required." When you give, it shows that you believe there's an unending supply of money, and it will never run out if you take care of it the right way. When you give, you have to believe that it will all come back to you, just like a boomerang.

My daughter-in-law Quinn and my grandson Julian volunteer with the Lowcountry Orphanage, which is a non-profit organization in Charleston that provides support services to children who suffer from abandonment, abuse, or neglect. My grandson gets to see first-hand that there is always someone who has it worse than you do; I believe that it's very important to instill these kinds of values in our children and youth. If your heart is in the right place, you will experience so much joy by giving some of what's been given to you.

Giving to charity has become such a big passion in my life. There are many causes I choose to support, but the fight against cancer is my number one. In 1991, I founded the McDaniels Automotive Group Golf Classic and Gala with all the proceeds initially benefitting Palmetto Health Hospital, and later, the Lexington Medical Center Foundation, as it still does today. I started the Classic in honor of my father, who battled with cancer, and it continues to be one of the biggest fund raisers for cancer in Columbia. In 1993, I joined the Palmetto Health Hospital Foundation and Cancer Board, where I served for six years and helped raise over $4 million. In 2014, I was Palmetto's signature sponsor and awarded the Order of the Palmetto—the highest philanthropic award to a civilian in the state—by then-Governor Nikki Haley.

When Suzanne came into my life, one of the things that bonded us was our intimate experience with cancer. Suzanne's first husband had passed away after a very tough battle with lym-

Receiving the Order of the Palmetto with former
SC Governor Nikki Haley and Suzanne

phoma. Emotionally, it's extremely difficult to sit back and watch your loved one waste away from this terrible disease. So, when the door opened for Suzanne to become involved with the Golf Classic, she jumped right into it because it was a way that we could both make an impact together, and it was very healing for both of us. We are in our third year of the McDaniels Golf Classic with Lexington Medical as the beneficiary. We've found that the more money we raise, the more driven we are to make the event bigger and better every year. After the event in 2020, we will have raised close to $2 Million with Lexington Medical Center, and close to $6 Million for Palmetto and Lexington combined.

This foundation is one of the best foundations in Columbia. With most foundations, the employees are paid based on the funds that are raised. Here, the hospital pays for all the salaries of the people who are working for the foundation; therefore, every dime that Lexington Medical Center raises is given back to the community by way of scholarships and other means. When you go to that hospital, you're treated like family.

Presenting the 2019 McDaniels Golf Classic proceeds
to Lexington Medical Center

"I don't know of any other organization that's raised more money than golf has, because if you are a baseball player, you're a football player, you're a hockey player, if you're just a businessman, and you want to raise some money for a charity, what do they do? They have a golf tournament. They have a golf outing, and they go out and they do it."

—*Lee Trevino*

Raising money for charity through golf is a win-win, because to me, there's no better sport. It's a way I can enjoy one of my favorite pastimes with family, friends, and the community while blessing the lives of thousands of people. Next to golf, I'm also a huge supporter of the University of South Carolina Gamecocks football, baseball, and basketball teams.

Supporting the Tiger Woods Foundation at Pebble Beach

Another charity we're passionate about is Leeza Gibbons' Dare2Care, which provides free support services to families with Alzheimer's and other types of chronic illness. Alzheimer's is also very near and dear to my heart, as I watched my mother lose her battle with this disease in 2003. Dare2Care operates like an adult daycare, where most of the volunteers are family members of loved ones who have died of Alzheimer's. Dare2Care currently serves over 250 families a week, connecting them with local resources and offering free support, education, and wellness programs.

I also support several community events for Fort Jackson Army Base, and my Subaru dealership is a primary supporter of the Bark to the Park charity for the Pawmetto Lifeline adoption of unwanted animals. (Suzanne and I have a soft spot for animals, as we have two cats, Baby Girl and Cooper, and a dog, Carmelo.)

> *"I don't want to live in the kind of world where we don't look out for each other. Not just the people that are close to us, but anybody who needs a helping hand. I can't change the way anybody else thinks, or what they choose to do, but I can do my bit."*
>
> —*Charles de Lint*

You may have had a childhood like mine—one of extreme poverty, dysfunction, hard times, and misfortunes. Does that mean you have to suffer a lackluster life? Absolutely not. What it *does* mean is that you'll probably need to spend your life working harder and doing more than someone who's grown up with a silver spoon in their mouth. That's just the way it is, and it's something I accepted a very long time ago. As the saying goes, "Everyone loves an underdog."

The "Cinderella Story" is the one where the downtrodden underdog rises from their humble beginnings and hardships to achieve greatness and glory in the end. Their life of struggle is the very thing that makes the end victory so sweet. Having personally lived this idea of a Cinderella Story, I can tell you, I have a feeling of gratitude, pride, and purpose that is beyond measure.

You might think that you'll start giving after you've made more money. I'm here to tell you, there's never a "good time" … just start doing it! Even if it's small. Simply getting into the habit of giving will open doors you can't imagine. No matter what you have to show for your life, it's important to take some time to glance in the rearview mirror to remember where you came from and acknowledge who helped you get you to where you are.

I believe that a person doesn't know how to live until they learn how to give; giving is my way of saying thank you for all that God has given to me. We all want to leave a legacy of a healthy family, a successful life, and leave the world in better shape than it was when we came into it. We do that not by the things we leave behind but by the way we live the moments we're given. To make a difference with your money doesn't mean you have to have a lot of it; it just means you have to find a way to contribute some of what you have. No matter how much or how little you have, you can use it in a way that affirms life rather than scrambling for more and obsessing about losing it. Money is a lot like water; it can come gushing into your life and flow like a big river or it can trickle in like a dripping faucet. Either way, you can pass it on in a way that will bless other peoples' lives. It's not about the amount you give, it's what you do with what you have.

I made the decision to choose a different path than the pain and struggle I grew up with, and I've never looked back. Where I came from drove me to choose a different journey. God had a purpose for me, and this is all part of it. I've made the most of the opportunities God has given to me, and I never want to take my success for granted.

At this stage in my life, I'm often asked, "What keeps you going?" and, "How much more money do you need?" The goal isn't to acquire more money for the sake of having it. The goal is being able to live life on my own terms, and the way I see it, the more money I make, the more I can give, and that's my biggest mission. Many people perceive it as greed, but it's not. There's a difference between ambition and greed. I believe that everything you do is for a purpose, and God has things for me to do and ways for me to serve; so, as long as I'm able, that's what I'm going to do. The truth is, everyone has a purpose, but most of the time, people just don't make it a point to figure out what it is, and they give up on life way too early. Ambition and hard work enable me to make a difference in this world, and to me, that's worth more than gold.

CHAPTER 8

HUGGING THE CURVES

I've got my seatbelt on and I'm ready to ride straight into the next phase of my life. I really don't know what it is... that's the exciting part.

I WISH I COULD SEE the future, but it would take all the excitement away if I could. At this point in my life, many people are thinking it's almost over but really, I'm just getting started!

What motivates me the most is having the opportunity to constantly be meeting new people, and that's what has always motivated me. I love selling cars. I love it when people call me and tell me what they want to drive, and it gives me so much joy when I see people's faces light up as they drive off with exactly what they wanted. When you've found something that you love to do, you naturally want to do more of it. Most people work all their life and hate what they're doing. I don't understand that—what a waste of the precious time that God has given them.

Another thing that motivates me to keep pushing is what I said about the consequences of making changes. When you make changes in life, you're not always sure how things are going to work out, but if you're afraid of moving forward, you can't be disappointed with an unfulfilled life. You have to be willing to take some risks. I've been fortunate to have achieved a lot in my life so far, but I haven't accomplished everything I'm meant to accomplish, that's for certain. I really think that the car business is just the beginning. It has put me in a position to meet people that influence other areas of my life, and I plan to explore how I can continue to make a difference in brand new ways.

Success isn't a destination. It's a state of mind that you live, exactly where you are.

As far as the car business goes, McDaniels Automotive Group will continue to expand throughout the East Coast. Within the next five years, we plan to double the dealerships from 6 to 12.

Within ten years, we'll expand to 20. Aggressive? Absolutely. The truth is, I could rest with the six dealerships I have now, but I know that I'm on a path to keep going. You have to! If you own just one dealership, you're already going out of business and just don't know it.

One of the things the car industry is experiencing in a huge way is digital marketing. The days of advertising on TV or in the newspapers are over. This is a perfect example of how you have to be ready to change and take risks. Never before have we had so much technological change to contend with. People are not jumping off the couch just because they saw a car ad on television. If you're not utilizing the advancements in technology and capitalizing on social media, you're already extinct.

At this point, we're building the best websites and doing a lot of work related to marketing to stay ahead of the game. Change is always happening; you have to be ready to change with it. And that change costs money! So, we have to keep growing.

I think part of being successful in life is really listening to people and being open to new ideas. I've never believed that I have all the answers, and that's part of why I value trust and strong relationships so much. That's what the car business is all about. I hear so many customers talk about being afraid of being taken advantage of or ripped off, and I hate that the industry often gets such a bad rap from the ones who do shady business. If I've learned anything, it's that success comes to those who are patient, trustworthy, and passionate about helping people, no matter what industry you're in.

You also can't let it go to your head when things are going well—you need to plan for the down slope the same way you plan for the upswing. It's not luck. There's nothing magical. It's just having the passion and ambition to wake up every day and do it all over again because you're making a difference. I've said that I don't like it when people ask me, "When is enough going to be enough?" because I'm making a difference in my own life and in other's lives, and I'll never get enough of that! I've come this far; I'm not about to waste any of the time God gives me.

MAKING AN IMPACT

I can't finish this book without stressing how greatly I've been im-pacted by GraceLife Church; serving the Christian community will continue to be an area that I find new ways to give back. You don't have to have a lot of money or be a preacher to influence people, but you do have to live your life in an upstanding way that's respected. From the lessons I've learned in my own spiri-tual journey, I know I can make a difference in the lives of others who are looking to be more successful in all areas of life—that's a path that I'm more excited about than anything because I know I wouldn't be alone. God says that all we have to do is believe in Him and He'll do the heavy lifting for us. Faith is everything, and if I can use my story to show just one person what's possible to achieve in their life, then that's what I'm going to do. I plan to go to Israel someday on a pilgrimage to experience an even deeper spiritual connection. In reconnecting with my faith, I've become a kinder person—more loving. I'm coming to grips with how I want my life to unfold, and the older I get, the more I feel like "the sky's the limit." I'm not the person I was yesterday, and I'm not the person I'll be tomorrow; that's the beauty of spiritual growth. You're always changing.

So, what drives me? A lot of things! I don't have all the answers as to what's coming next in my life; I just know when I get up, I'm going to make a difference in who I am now and who I want to be. I can't wait to open my eyes every morning so I can say, "Thank You, Jesus, for letting me have one more day." I'm not going to waste any of the time He gives me, and I feel like retiring and sitting on the couch, well… that's just not going to happen. I have to go out there and take on the next project and keep moving forward.

Big dreams usually have small beginnings.

Many people who have overcome a lot in their lives find it difficult to look in the rearview mirror because the past can hold some pretty painful memories. I'm no different. Deciding to get out of the environment I endured as a child was stressful to say the least. I was leaving my family and the only life I knew when I boarded that bus headed for Thomasville. I forced myself out of my comfort zone because I had to. I just knew there was more for me out there.

When I really made up my mind to write this book, I knew that I had to go back to my small beginnings. I remembered a lot from my childhood, but it had been many years since I'd visited Mullins and Floyds. I wanted to go back to those roots one more time, even though I knew it would cause me to dig up more memories that have been long left behind in my mind. I planned a two-day road trip that would start by touring Mullins, Floyds, and Nichols, SC—where it all began. Then, I would swing up through Thomasville and Greensboro, NC.

In 2017-2018, when I was renovating the Audi store in Charleston as well as doing a complete remodel of the Acura store there, I got a chance to spend a couple nights a week with Rob, Quinn, and Julian. Quinn played an instrumental role in the completion of those construction projects, helping with the finances and accounting, and I'm grateful for the way she contributed. As for Julian, I think I spent more time with him in those two years than I have in his whole lifetime. It was probably one of the best times I could've ever chosen to spend with him because I was fortunate to watch him grow into his teenage years, which is such an important time in a young man's life.

I witnessed the amount of poise and grace that Quinn had during this time of Julian's life, and it was remarkable to see the progress in his thinking patterns and behaviors. She is truly a caring, special woman and mother. He really came out of his shell, and I realized what a brilliant young man he is. He had started to dig into his family tree for a school project and was learning a lot about his ancestry, and he and I spent many hours together talking about our family heritage and tracing things back as far as I could remember. With the technology available today, he was able to trace back about four generations, and he now has pictures of my great-grandparents and knows more details about my ancestry than I do. Another thing that happened in that process was Julian found out that Rob was not my biological son, and he discovered who his biological grandfather was. This opened the discussion about my adopting Rob when Julian was about two years old.

When I decided to take my road trip, I invited Julian to ride along with me. Now, most 15-year-olds wouldn't be all that excited about taking a two-day road trip with their grandfather, but with all the work he had done to piece together the puzzle of our family tree, I think he was kind of looking forward to visiting those roots of where it all began. On June 18, 2019, we hit the road and made our way to Mullins. We drove "downtown," which hadn't changed much. Most of the factories, including the textile mill where mother folded t-shirts, had been long abandoned, and the town didn't have much of a buzz at all. Life seemed about as slow as I remembered it there. On the square sits the SC Tobacco Museum, which was unfortunately closed that day, but I was able to share with Julian how the tobacco industry was what kept Mullins alive. We talked about what it was like to work on the family tobacco farms as a young boy. We also visited the cemetery

Visiting the SC Tobacco Museum

in Nichols to pay respects to our many family members who are buried there, including my mother, father, and siblings.

From there, we drove through to Nichols, SC, which was even more destitute. Nichols had been severely hit by floods in recent years, and there were more abandoned houses than we could count. It was astounding and very sad. Most of the businesses had closed down as well, showing very little signs of an economic pulse. Then, we drove by Free Welcome Pentecostal Holiness Church, where I dusted pews as a boy. The church was locked up, but boy, did I have a lot of memories in that place. The old schoolhouse that I grew up in across the street had been torn down and replaced by a mobile home.

We drove past the jailhouse, and I told Julian a story about the time my brother John got thrown in jail for drinking and fighting. All that was left were a few broken concrete walls overgrown by weeds, but he got a kick out of that. Then, it was on to the one-stoplight town of Floyds. There, we drove past my grandparents' old farm properties and visited the tiny cemetery where more of our family had been laid to rest.

My old schoolhouse home

The next stop was Thomasville, NC to revisit my high school, the grocery stores where I worked to help keep food on the table, and the places we lived, including that first house that I bought on Ferndale Drive and several of the houses I had built with Pat. It was interesting to see how Thomasville has decayed, much in the same way Mullins has. What was once the furniture capital now had just a bunch of empty, run-down furniture factories. We spent the following day in the Greensboro area visiting the car dealerships where I got my start in the business, and then headed back to Columbia.

Nichols Jailhouse

Thomasville, NC Chair

It was important for me to show Julian where I came from and what you can do with your life if you make the right decisions at the right time. I couldn't be prouder of the brilliant young man he's becoming, and I'll always remember that trip and what a delight it was to have him along.

> *"I see my path, but I don't know where it leads. Not knowing where I'm going is what inspires me to travel it."*
> —*Rosalia de Castro*

I can't change where I've been, but I can sure change where I'm going. With everything I do, I try to look in the rearview mirror to see where I've missed opportunities and then figure out how I can make it better. But I don't look in that mirror for very long.

Thomasville High School

A quick glance is all it takes, because you can't continue to live in the past if you want to have a successful future. There's no point in living with a bunch of "what ifs." You're going to make some bad decisions, and the best thing you can do is learn from them and do things differently the next time. With every situation, there's a devil sitting on one shoulder and an angel sitting on the other. Bad decisions will lead to unwanted results, which will promote more bad decisions. Before long, you'll find yourself wondering how in the world you got where you are. Good decisions may not be as thrilling in the moment, but they make life really exciting down the line. I'm living proof of that.

Aside from the things I have in my vision, I don't think much about tomorrow; it's much more important to experience today. I want to enjoy what's happening right now. I'm excited about the

Fast Stop, formerly Florida Markets grocery store

future because I know that if I'm patient, the right people and opportunities will come. I pray that I'll live until at least 2050—that gives me another three decades to open doors and make a difference.

I don't know how the next chapter of my life is going to turn out, but I've got my seatbelt on and I'm ready to ride. I expect there to be a few bumps and a whole lot of excitement because I believe we can accomplish anything we want—and believe me, I still have a lot to do! So, ask me now when enough is enough, and I'll tell you, "I can rest when I die."

CONCLUSION

MAKE THE RIDE UNFORGETTABLE

THE LIFE YOU LIVE IS THE LEGACY YOU LEAVE

Sometimes I sit back and wonder how I've made it this far. It all comes back to those choices and decisions. It's easy to look back on your life and focus on your mistakes, but what we perceive to be a mistake is just God trying to get our attention and put us back on the path we should be on. In writing this book, I've been challenged to look at a lot of things that I could say were mistakes, but the reality is, even though God has a plan for our lives, He allows us to go out there and wander. He gives us the ability to choose which path we want to be on every single day. My biggest joy in life has been seeing where I made a wrong turn, hit a dead end, and how I had to turn right back around and keep on driving.

We are all influenced by our environment, our family and friends, where we grew up, where we live, where we work, and the people we surround ourselves with. When we choose to visualize our dreams and work like crazy to achieve them, we live a life of incredible accomplishment and abundance. I've learned that you can control your attitude about what happens in your life, and the attitude you choose impacts the decisions you make. Those decisions ultimately determine the outcomes of your life.

For every bad decision I made in my life, there were two good ones, and those are the ones I choose to focus on. When you can learn how to find the good that comes from your bad decisions, you're on your way to real happiness. I could say that my failed marriages were mistakes, but instead, I choose to see the good: my incredible children, Tracey and Rob. I could say the amount of time I spent building a family business was a mistake, but instead, I choose to see the good: I'm leaving a legacy through

McDaniels Automotive Group that will benefit my family for many generations to come.

On his death bed, my father told me, "I'm only 59… I just started living, I'm not ready to go. There are so many things I want to change." That moment changed my life. When my time comes, the only thing I want to say is, "What an unforgettable ride my life has been."

The thing is, you have to start early. You can't work forever, and you never know how long your health will support you, so the sooner you decide to make positive choices that will produce the results you want to see in your life, the more time you have to create the kind of ride you want to have. If after reading this book, you're still wondering how you can make the most of the life you've lived up to this point, just remember that it's never too late to reinvent yourself. If you change the way you think about your life, the benefits become very personal. Your business will change, your relationships will change, and you'll enjoy a satisfaction with life that's deeper than you could ever imagine.

Growing up, I was living life to simply survive and exist. When you're born in that kind of environment, there's nothing pushing you to be successful. It's perfectly acceptable to stay in your comfort zone and never have the desire for more—and more importantly, the guts to go out and get it. When no one else believed in me, I made the decision to believe in myself. If I had grown up with a silver spoon in my mouth, my life would've been entirely different. But the way I grew up taught me a lot about life; along the way, I learned what's really important, and you don't have to wait until you're on your death bed to figure that out. Time stops for no one. I knew where I wanted to go, and I knew that path wouldn't be easy. I knew the life I wanted would require a lot of sacrifice, and today, I wouldn't trade it for the world. If I had it to do all over, I might take a few different turns, but the road I've traveled has made me who I am today. I'm at peace with myself. I'm balanced. And that's a great place to be.

> *Don't let your current situation determine your final destination.*

God has given me a life far beyond anything I could've ever dreamed. When I took a step, He took two. Sometimes you don't quite understand what is happening in your life, but you still have to take responsibility for it. At some point, you made a decision that guided you in that direction, whether you like it or not. And I think where many people get lost is that they don't realize that it's never too late to make some new decisions that redirect you onto the path that you really want. One small decision you can make is to simply start being nicer to people. When I walk by someone, I smile at them and say hello. I make a point to connect with them, even if it's just through the energy I share with them. I want people to feel good as a result of having met me, so I carry myself in a way that's open and inviting.

DECIDE ON YOUR RIDE

> *"A dream without ambition is like a car without gas; you're not going anywhere."*
> —*Sean Hampton*

Decide to see the silver lining that's under the surface of challenges and adversities. When it feels like life is giving you lemons, squeeze them, look for the lesson, add a little sugar, and make some lemonade. I never thought I would achieve what I've achieved in my life because with every goal I set, God not only met me there,

He took it to a level I hadn't even imagined. Taking something bad and turning it into something good has been one of the most valuable lessons of my life. Put your dreams into action by creating a vision and setting goals that will help you get there.

Decide to make a difference. Most people would rather sit on the couch and watch some crappy TV than try to go out and do something to make a difference. Dusting pews as a young boy may not seem like a huge deal, but I know it made a difference to the people who showed up to worship on Sunday morning. There's no halo around my head, but I do understand the value and importance of giving in order to receive. And to be fair, I've made a lot of conscious, intentional changes to get there. I didn't simply say, "I'd like to make a change;" I actually had to go out there and make change happen.

Decide what you stand for. Growing up, one of my idols was Elvis Presley, and one of my favorite songs is "He Touched Me." Everything that I've accomplished has been from a combination of my own hard work and God's helpful, benevolent touch. I try to live my life in a principle-based way that you can't miss. From

My home in Elgin, SC

generosity and giving to charities, to the way I treat my colleagues and employees, to meeting the needs of others first, I want to be celebrated as a God-fearing man who made one helluva difference while I was on this Earth. You've got to know what you stand for in life and then be willing to work toward those things in order to become the best version of yourself. It doesn't just happen miraculously. God helps people who help themselves.

Decide to be grateful. I try very hard to put God first because that will inevitably take care of the rest of what goes on in my life. I give thanks every morning with a very simple prayer:

"Thank you, God for giving me this day. I promise I will not waste it. Thank you for sending your only Son so my sins could be forgiven. Please guide me through the day to live the life that you want me to live. Amen." And at night, it's "I thank you for this day. Thank you for taking care of my family and thank you for all your blessings." And then I go to sleep. I don't believe that prayer needs to be long and drawn out; God already knows the true nature of our hearts. But anyone will tell you that the key to manifesting an abundant life is to start with gratitude for what you've been given, not by asking for everything you want. God already knows what you want and is always listening.

Decide to reinvent yourself. No matter what you're going through, you have the power and the choice to change your life. It's never too late. You can decide to be happy. You have the choice to begin every day with a pleasant attitude and demeanor, and your energy speaks to every person you encounter. You attract people who are most like you. What do the people in your life say about who you are? Decide to be confident in who you are. See yourself as confident, even if there are areas where you aren't. Practice speaking to people using a strong posture and self-assured language. This isn't to put on a facade or false persona; it will actually help you strengthen your abilities and push through the fears and doubts that subconsciously try to hold you back.

Decide to live the life of your dreams. I don't know what the final plan is, but whatever it is, I'm good with it—I'm sure it'll be something fantastic. Sometimes you have to wander out there to really appreciate what's in your life right now. Recognizing the contrast of what you've been through in life gives you more to appreciate. We all have battles every day. We have a lot to accomplish, and we've got time to do it. So, there is no going home and sitting down on the couch—at least not for me. My aim is putting the pedal to the metal and getting the job done.

Decide to forgive. You have to forgive your family for their mistakes and ask for forgiveness where you need it. If there's been one hero in my life, it was my mother. She taught me about values through her actions, not her words: being kind-hearted, generous, and unselfish. I wish she had been around longer to see what I've accomplished here on Earth; I think she'd be proud. Mother taught me to love people and to forgive them, no matter what. Although I've made mistakes along the way, I wanted to have that foundation of pure love of family, and I hope my family knows they can always count on me.

BUCKLE UP

I find it truly amazing to see where my journey started and where it is now. I don't know if there's a word in the dictionary to describe what I've achieved, but I couldn't have imagined a life that's much better than this. What has been my favorite chapter in life so far? Maybe the first one... because of the innocence in having no idea what I could do or who I could be. What I could have. Where I could live. To come from not having anything to where I am today, it's truly unbelievable. I don't fully know God's plan for me, but I know the more I'm out there willing to serve, the more

He'll use me. Wherever the path leads, the most important thing is that we're driving in the same direction.

I hope this book inspires you in some way to buckle up and make the decision to live tomorrow in a way that's better than yesterday. It costs you nothing to dream and everything not to. And it's the ride of your life, so you might as well make it unforgettable.

ABOUT THE AUTHOR

Bill McDaniels has worked in the automotive industry since 1969 and is the President, Owner, and Founder of McDaniels Automotive Group in South Carolina, which includes McDaniels Acura of Columbia and Charleston, McDaniels Porsche, McDaniels Subaru, McDaniels Volkswagen of Columbia, and McDaniels Audi of Charleston. He is the former Chairman of The National Dealer Council, as well as the Honda Finance National Advisory Committee for Acura.

In 2011, Bill was recognized as Fundraiser of the Year by the Association of Fundraising Professionals. In 2013, he was named Donor of the Year by The Midlands Foundation for Foster Children. He has served as a member of the Columbia Executives & Owners Association for 13 years.

In 2014, Bill received the Order of the Palmetto from former South Carolina Governor, Nikki Haley, the highest philanthropic award given to a civilian in the state. He was also honored with the Silver Leaf Award for Community Service by former South Carolina Lt. Governor, Andre Bauer.

Bill served 6 years on the Palmetto Health Hospital Cancer Board and Palmetto Health Hospital Foundation and was inducted in the Palmetto Health Foundations Fellows for exemplary service, leadership, and personal commitment to the foundation.

Through his annual McDaniels Golf Classic and Gala, Bill has raised almost $6 Million to support the battle against cancer.

In the past 3 years, he has partnered with the Lexington Medical Center Foundation, which has raised almost $2 Million.

As a corporate sponsor, McDaniels Automotive Group has been a Golden Eagle sponsor for the Honda Golf Classic for 30 years. McDaniels Subaru is the primary sponsor of Pawmetto Lifeline's Bark in the Park event for the adoption of unwanted animals. McDaniels is a strong supporter of the University of South Carolina's football, basketball, and baseball teams, as well as multiple community activities supporting Fort Jackson Army Base.

Bill is a licensed general contractor in North Carolina and South Carolina, an active member and supporter of GraceLife Church in Columbia, and he enjoys spending time with his family and on the golf course.